Let Us Keep the Feast

Let Us Keep the Feast

Celebrating Lent, Holy Week, and Easter

Kevin Flynn
editor

A Liturgy Canada Book

Published and distributed by

Anglican Book Centre
Toronto, Canada

1998
Anglican Book Centre
600 Jarvis Street
Toronto, Ontario
M4Y 2J6

Cover illustration: "The Last Supper," Ugolino di Nerio

Canadian Cataloguing in Publication Data

Let us keep the feast: celebrating Lent, Holy Week, and Easter

ISBN 1-55126-191-X

1. Anglican Church of Canada – Liturgy. 2. Lent. 3. Holy week.
4. Easter.
I. Flynn, Kevin (Kevin W.)

BX5616.L47 1998 264'.03 C98-930023-4

Contents

Introduction 7
Lent and the New Liturgy: A Pastoral Perspective 16

Liturgies of the Lenten Season 41
Ash Wednesday 42
A Penitential Order 47

Holy Week 51
The Sunday of the Passion with the Liturgy of the Palms 52
Monday, Tuesday, and Wednesday in Holy Week 63

The Triduum: The Great Three Days 65
Maundy Thursday 66
Good Friday 74
Holy Saturday 81
The Great Vigil of Easter 85

The Great Fifty Days 103
The Sundays of Eastertide 104
The Vigil of the Resurrection for Saturday Evenings 110
The Vigil of Pentecost 116

Music for the Paschal Celebration 120
Glossary 134
For Further Reading 139
Music List 141
Contributors 142

INTRODUCTION

Everyone wants worship to come alive. We all know that the words on the pages of *The Book of Alternative Services* are most fully realized when they are said or sung by a worshipping community, gathered for the purpose of celebrating the mysteries to which the texts point. This book is meant to serve as a guide to communities hoping to celebrate and deepen the faith of the church as represented in the rites of *The Book of Alternative Services.*

The book provides a background to the history and theology of the rites of Lent, Holy Week, and Easter, and explains the rationale for the new look that the *BAS* gives to these seasons, as it draws from the inspiration and practice of biblical and patristic sources mediated through the Anglican tradition. The text includes narrative descriptions of ceremonial that can attend the celebration of the rites, which may prove useful for communities planning their worship.

It may be helpful, here at the outset, to distinguish between two related terms: *rite* (or ritual) and *ceremonial.* Strictly speaking, the rites are those prescribed sets of texts and directions found in such authorized books as *The Book of Common Prayer* and *The Book of Alternative Services*. Ceremonial, on the other hand, refers to the actions that accompany these rites. The Eucharistic Prayer, for example, belongs to the rite; the use of incense, on the other hand, is a matter of ceremonial. Thus, while Anglican communities inevitably have common rites, the ceremonial may vary enormously from place to place. This guide deals with both.

For over a decade, Anglican Christians in Canada have been celebrating the central seasons of the liturgical year with the rites of *The Book of Alternative Services.* The *BAS* brings together, in a coherent and authorized way, many practices that have been in use throughout the Canadian church for years. Great variations of church architecture, local tradition, and congregational size and resources throughout the Anglican Church of Canada mean that there is no one way in which the rites are celebrated. Everyone involved in liturgical planning and celebration, however, will benefit from an understanding of the history of our various practices, an appreciation of the logic of a season or a day, and the details of a particular rite. This book emerges from the conviction that those rites may be used thoughtfully, joyfully, and with integrity to celebrate the death and rising of Jesus Christ, the Paschal Mystery. May it help worship come alive in your particular setting!

In its concern with ceremonial, this guide offers suggestions about details for the organization of the service, movements and roles of the various ministers, and matters relating to altar guilds and others. (A useful adjunct resource is *Servers and Services: Instructions for Serving Anglican Liturgies*, which, in its consideration of differing parish situations, provides directions for both spare and complex liturgical actions.) Services described here may envision a larger cast of characters than your congregation is used to including. Not every parish has torchbearers, thurifers, and so on. Sometimes the extent of the ceremonial depends on available volunteers; sometimes a simpler celebration is the custom. These descriptions, then, are not prescriptive; rather, they are intended as helpful reminders about the range of liturgical ministers who might be involved.

There are a number of presuppositions at work in this guide. First is the conviction that worship matters and that those who are charged with its stewardship do well to take it seriously. This is perhaps so obvious as to appear a pointless platitude. But for the vast majority of Anglicans, the Sunday experience is their only occasion of encounter with the gospel. This book assumes that the encounter in the Sunday assembly is formative — which is not to say that, if we somehow just "get the liturgy right," all will be well with the church. The liturgy does not stand on its own, divorced from any connection with catechesis, private prayer, work for justice, or any other crucial aspect of the church's life. Nevertheless, the church is a "story-formed community." It is rooted in the Paschal Mystery. As Christians together encounter this story week by week, they meet the primary witness to all that is foundational for their common life.

The reading of Scripture in the faith community has the effect, over time, of irrigating the imaginations of the faithful, and thus shaping our perceptions of faith and reality. So convinced are Christians that the Scriptures are a means of encountering God, that these texts are almost invariably surrounded by song. From psalmody to short ecstatic outbursts such as "Alleluia!" and "Glory to you, Lord Jesus Christ!" the proclamation of Scripture is bounded about by song. Singing gives voice to the deep sense that here a new thing is happening, that the ancient texts will speak a fresh word. Preaching seeks to relate the primordial witness to the present life of the church, and so includes the community in the continuing story of God's work in the world. Christians, then, live between memory and hope — the memory of what God has done in the past gives hope for what God will do, even through us, in the future.

But the reading of Scripture does not stand alone. It is bounded about by a series of ritual actions that arise from, and point to, the saving Word. Rituals embody the story of the community and define that community's boundaries. While most Anglicans will never undertake the systematic study of theology, all have access to a primary mode of "doing theology," namely, the liturgy. What and how we pray is a fundamental liturgical and theological catechesis. It is through rituals such as bathing and eating, speaking and listening, anointing and clothing that the Christian vision of life is represented. The rites invite people to join themselves anew to that vision: they reinforce the community's sense of identity and relatedness to one another, to God, and to the world.

The renewed rites for Lent, Holy Week, and Easter have the potential of opening, informing, and enriching the faithful, and of drawing individuals and communities beyond themselves into more faithful living. The chapter entitled "Lent and the New Liturgy" presents the theological vision that undergirds the Paschal cycle. In preparing to celebrate the seasons, key members of the liturgical team would do well to become familiar with this overall vision.

For the purposes of this guide, it will be assumed that those responsible for planning and leading the liturgy share a deep commitment to the formative character of worship. Whatever the resources available to us, we are all called to excellence. This most certainly does not mean that every parish will try to reproduce a cathedral-style service in its own setting! But a commitment to excellence will honour and take seriously the people, place, and traditions of a given community. Each chapter in this book provides background to the particular celebrations of Lent and Easter, and checklists for the "holy hardware" that may be needed. Not every community will make use of all that might be done on a given occasion. But it is hoped that planning teams will take the suggestions in this book, adapt them to their situation, and find still fresher approaches to celebration. Different solutions will apply in each situation.

A brief quotation from one of the Fathers of the church begins each major section of the book. The world of the Fathers is, of course, very far removed from ours in many ways. Those unfamiliar with the rhetorical style of these authors may, at first, find them difficult to interpret. The quotations are included, however, because they derive from an era that may be described as "the springtime of the liturgy." These writers were first and foremost pastors whose characteristic place of instruction was the liturgy. They lived at a time of enormous liturgical and devotional fruitfulness, when the shape and spirit of the rites we have inherited were first coming into being. Brief as these quotations are, they may serve to stimulate some reflection on the season or occasion to be celebrated, or even encourage further reading![1]

---

1 There are various translations and collections of patristic writers. Please see the brief bibliography in "For Further Reading" should you wish to read further in this area. Selections in this book are the editor's translations from Migne's *Patrologia Latina* and *Patrologia Graeca*.

This guide assumes that planning will involve a number of people. Consider which key people or groups in your parish help your worship come to life. They will likely include clergy, musicians, greeters, members of the altar guild, servers, readers, intercessors, and ministers of communion. In some places a number of these roles may be combined. The planning process could well incorporate representatives from each group early on, so that the perspectives and concerns of as wide a range of people as possible are brought to bear.

Planning cannot be left to only the clergy and, perhaps, the organist. This guide's theological presupposition is that the chief minister of the liturgy is none other than the assembly itself, and that all other liturgical ministries are to serve that primary ministry.[2] What does this mean? Someone has said that in the liturgy we used to think of the priest as actor, God as prompter, and the congregation as audience. To say that the chief minister of the liturgy is the assembly is to revise that view drastically. It would perhaps be more fitting to say that the *assembly* is the actor, the priest is the prompter, and God is the audience! Planning, then, is more than a matter of fitting a few hymns into "the usual places." Planning must enable the members of the Body of Christ, gathered in a particular place and time, to participate fully in doing its liturgy. In practice, this requires a number of considerations.

Some communities find it valuable to have a regular Bible study group that reads in advance the lections for a coming Sunday. Preachers report that such groups stimulate and aid their preparation for the Sunday homily. Planning for Lent and Easter, however, requires a preparation lead-time that is more than just a Sunday or a celebration ahead. A planning team for Lent and Eastertide could be invited to read the seasons' texts in advance of

---

[2] See David R. Holeton, ed., "Principles and Recommendations," in *Our Thanks and Praise: The Eucharist in Anglicanism Today: Papers from the Fifth International Anglican Liturgical Consultation.* Toronto: Anglican Book Centre, 1998.

its first meeting, and come prepared to discuss a selection of key texts. Alternately, they might begin with reflection on the crucial and extended narratives of the Passion and Resurrection, and work outward from there, considering how these texts might be speaking to the community *this* year, and so giving shape to the time of preparation leading up to the Great Three Days, or *Triduum*, as well as the season of Resurrection that flows from them.

How long before Lent should planning begin? This will vary from place to place, depending on such factors as the date of Easter, the parish traditions that influence what normally takes place, the amount of new music (if any) that has to be learned, and the number of people involved in planning. Ideally, the broad outline of how a congregation will celebrate the season should be in place *before* the season starts.

Whatever the approach, the essential ingredient is time — time to ponder individually and together such questions as, "What are these readings saying to me? To our community? To the wider church? To the world? What is the good news here?" Do particular images or concerns dominate the group's reflection? Might these suggest particular symbolic actions or offer guidance as to how the environment might be arranged or decorated for the celebrations? A member of the group might be designated as secretary, so that ideas can be recorded for future reference.

When planning, consideration should be given to who will be at our celebrations. Are we planning for several hundred people or several dozens? What age groups will attend? Will there be some with special needs or disabilities that must be accommodated? Do those attending have a memory of celebrating this rite before? What did we do last year and the year before that? Can we build on certain elements of our tradition? What might we eliminate from, or add to, our celebrations?

Another consideration is the weather. What might the weather be like? What sort of clothing do we wear at this time of year? When does daylight-saving time start this year? What crucial issues are facing our town or city or country at this time? What kinds of issues might be weighing on people's minds?

How will our liturgical space help us to serve the people? The environment of the liturgy has a profound effect on how people relate to one another, and on their ability to share in the symbolic actions of the liturgy. Whatever the limitations on the flexibility of our space, careful thought should be given to such things as optimum seating arrangements, acoustical properties of the space, and sight lines. Can any improvements be made well in advance of the season? It might be time to suggest, for instance, taking up the carpet that so deadens the sound! Flowers, banners, fabric art, and the like can be considered for use by those planning the liturgy. Even with limited resources, the transition to a new season or celebration can be made immediately obvious through a few deft changes to the decoration of the worship space. In one rural church, for example, large wreaths made of grapevines are decked with poinsettias and ivy at Christmas, and with lilies at Easter.

As these questions are considered, specific ideas for music, decoration, preaching, and so on will begin to emerge. It might be a good idea to pause from time to time as individual services are sketched out, to consider whether the rhythmic flow of the service will be maintained. Is one section of the service overweighed by too much music? Is another dominated by a lot of talk? Could silence or some meditative music be introduced at appropriate places? Planning teams should be attentive to the relative importance of elements of the rite. They should be encouraged to recognize the natural rhythms of the liturgy.

The beginning and end of the liturgy are notorious "soft spots" where a superfluity of material often builds up. We can so overload the gathering and sending of the community that the primary purpose is lost. It is not necessary, for example, to include in the gathering rite a processional hymn, a choir anthem, the Gloria, and "Lord, have mercy." Similarly, the dismissal in the *BAS* is quite spare, with a prayer of thanks for the fruits of communion and a doxology, followed by words of dismissal. There is no need here for any additional elements.

Plan to build the momentum as the liturgy approaches certain climactic points. In the Liturgy of the Word, for example, the climax is the proclamation of the Gospel. In the Liturgy of the Sacrament, the highlight is the Great Thanksgiving.

Another consideration is the mental and emotional space people need to appropriate the richness of the texts heard during these festivals. If silence (after the Bible readings, for instance) has not been a part of your church's celebrations up to now, Lent may be a good opportunity to help parishioners develop a capacity for it.

This guide occasionally refers to particular postures or gestures that may accompany some of the actions of the liturgy. As ever, parish custom varies enormously. Anglican worship in our part of the world tends to be fairly restrained in its use of the body as an instrument for expressing prayer. Even so, we are familiar with standing, sitting, and kneeling as common postures at different points in the liturgy. The *BAS* recovers for Anglicans the option of standing for prayer. This was the posture used by Christians in the Western church well into the high Middle Ages, until it was replaced largely by kneeling. Many other Christian traditions have never abandoned standing to pray.

Many of us grew up seeing the ordained person standing to pray while the rest of us knelt. A quite different expression of the relation of the ordained to the laity results when *all* stand to pray during the eucharistic prayer, for example. People may wish to explore this ancient posture more fully by assuming the *orans* position for the hands and arms. The faithful in the Western church stood thus to pray for many centuries, until the increasing clericalization of the church gave rise to significantly different stances and gestures during the course of the liturgy.

In some parishes, the clergy reverence the altar as a symbol of Christ, on entering or leaving the chancel or sanctuary. Consider the possibility of the clergy then turning and reverencing the congregation with a similar profound bow, as the *other* principal symbol of Christ in the building. No explanation is necessary. Within a very short while, members of the congregation will begin to bow back. This practice can become customary throughout the year.

Finally, the planning team needs to ensure that all involved in the services receive clear instructions about when they will be needed for rehearsals, set-up, preparation, or whatever. In some cases, budgeting may be necessary, perhaps a year in advance, so that new vestments or hangings can be purchased as needed.

It might seem that, after two thousand years of Christian worship, we should have no problems "getting it right." But getting it right is always a matter of "more or less" because so many variables come into play in the celebration of a liturgy. At the completion of a celebration or a liturgical season, the planning team should be invited to evaluate what went well, what did not, and what was merely indifferent. It would be useful to record these insights for next year's planning. Ultimately, of course, we cannot compel the Spirit. We can only so arrange things and dispose ourselves as to be open to the Spirit's movement throughout the liturgy.

Lent and the New Liturgy

A Pastoral Perspective

One of the significant liturgical reforms that has taken place in the Anglican Church of Canada over the past several decades, and which is being incorporated into the pastoral renewal of the liturgical life of many parishes, is the celebration of the central mystery of our redemption — the annual celebration of the *Pasch* (the Paschal Mystery) — and the liturgical period that surrounds it, the time spanning Ash Wednesday to Pentecost.

One way of gaining a perspective on our present celebration of Lent, Holy Week, and Eastertide is to reflect on what things were like a quarter of a century ago.

In those days Lent felt to me as if it began on Septuagesima, when the liturgical colour changed to purple and hymnody took on a more serious character. Ash Wednesday (invariably without ashes in most churches) seemed to come almost mid-course. Many of us were given Lenten cards into which we put the daily quarter, a large sum of money then. A Lent of considerably more than forty days of "giving up something" followed.

On the fifth Sunday in Lent, we began Passiontide, although on Passion Sunday we didn't read the Passion, except at Evening Prayer. In some churches the main features that made the season different were the change in the liturgical colour from purple to red and the processional cross draped in a purple shroud. The cross on the altar was now only vaguely discernible through a similar draping made of what appeared to be purple gossamer.

On the next Sunday, Palm Sunday, we did hear the Passion, but the palms from which this Sunday took its name were not given any liturgical significance. Either they were distributed on trays by a server who sometimes followed the priest while he was administering the chalice, or they were handed to members of the congregation as they left the church. Instead of providing whole palm branches, which the crowds had spread before Jesus on his triumphal entry into Jerusalem, they used an Anglican version of the holy card or bookmark — palm fronds that had been woven into small crosses by the altar guild.

Holy Week was a period of intense religious activity. At the eucharist, from Monday to Thursday, we read our way through all the Passions. On Thursday evening, we celebrated the eucharist to commemorate the institution of the Holy Communion, an event that seemed to be marked by no particular rite or ceremony to distinguish it as an especially significant celebration. Its only defining feature was the change of liturgical colour from red to white. Some parishes kept all-night vigils at which people kept up their strength with hot cross buns and strong coffee.

On Good Friday a parish might have Matins, Litany, Ante-Communion; visiting English bishops preaching on the Seven Last Words; and a Choir Spectacular. This all-day event was punctuated by hymns, during which people could slip in and out. The liturgical events of the day were the least popular, while the extra-liturgical ones, such as Stations of the Cross, attracted the biggest attendance.

Then there was a breather. No services until Easter day, unless you happened to visit the one parish in the city that celebrated the Vigil. This event I recall as being very long, very late, and liturgically very chaste, with very little liturgical action except among the clergy. The new fire made only a faint glow from behind the pillar where it was kindled, and the "baptismal" water was sprinkled most sparingly. Indeed, there were never any baptisms.

Easter morning was quite obviously *the* event of the week. Everybody was there, new hats all aflourish. But except for the readings, hymns, liturgical colour, and immense floral display, the liturgy itself was virtually identical to that of the preceding Sunday. And there was no question about the possibility of baptizing anyone at Easter.

Easter Sunday was followed by a series of events, many of which seemed only tenuously related to Easter. The Prayer Book propers for Monday and Tuesday after Easter (the only weekdays for which provision was made), and those of "the Octave Day of Easter: being the Sunday after Easter Day," were quite obviously related to Easter. Otherwise, the proper prayers and readings appeared to take an independent turn, or else were related to the festivals of the Ascension (followed by Ascensiontide) or Whitsunday, which was itself given an octave. This series of apparently independent festivals ended on Trinity Sunday.

Recalling these Lents of the not too distant past and remembering their observances, it is notable how much things have changed in the present liturgical practice of most Anglican parishes. The pre-Lenten Sundays have disappeared from the calendar, and Lent now clearly begins on Ash Wednesday, for which occasion ashes have found their way into most parishes.

Today, it is probable that many people have given up "giving up" during Lent. Passiontide has disappeared, and the particular ceremonies of Passion or Palm Sunday, Maundy Thursday, Good Friday, and Holy Saturday have won a place in the liturgies of most parishes. The great Fifty Days from Easter to Pentecost are once again, as in the era of their first development, an integral whole. A clear theological or pastoral overview of Lent, Holy Week, the *Triduum*, or the Fifty Days of Eastertide, as these times are now celebrated in the life of the church, is called for. To do this we will need to make a short historical excursus that will put both past and present observances into perspective.

Liturgical Development: Evolution and Devolution

As in no other age since the Reformation of the sixteenth century, liturgical renewal in our time has been dominated by a search for historical roots. This is not a vain search for a golden age that can, in some way, be recapitulated and imposed on the church. Rather, it is a serious attempt to discover how things came to be the way they are, so that we can come to know the relative antiquity, value, theological significance, and pastoral importance of the constituent pieces of the liturgy. With this knowledge, it is hoped that we can develop the ability to judge which of those pieces should be retained, which might be usefully restored, and which might be let go for the sake of an integral and theologically justifiable whole, so that the church, the whole People of God, might best be equipped for its true work of proclaiming the gospel afresh in our own age.

Here, the much-used adage is particularly true: *Lex orandi statuit lex credendi*. The law of prayer does constitute the law of belief. Our practice informs doctrine. The difficulty is that Lent, as it was inherited and retained by the reformers who drafted the first Prayer Books, had little to do either with the historical origins of Lent and Eastertide or with the present need for reform to best equip us for our contemporary mission. The dissonance between the *lex orandi* and the *lex credendi* had reached a point that demanded thorough reform, if there was to be genuine renewal of the liturgical life of the church as the source and sustenance of its ministry of reconciliation and justice.

How does contemporary liturgical scholarship help us in this pursuit of renewal? We have learned that, in the first centuries of the church, a variety of practices obtained in the observance of the *Pasch*.[3] The forty-day Lent that emerged in the mid-fourth century was derived from a short fast of one to three and, later, six days linked to the *Pasch*. The Easter season, the Fifty Days (the eschatological week of weeks[4]), was an integrated period of particular joy culminating in Pentecost, the fiftieth day. As Sunday stood in relation to the week, so the Fifty Days stood in relation to the year.

The Paschal *Triduum* comprised what we call Good Friday, Holy Saturday, and Easter Day. These are the days Ambrose

---

3 The most recent and thorough study of the development of Pasch is found in Thomas J. Talley, *The Origins of the Liturgical Year* (New York: Pueblo, 1986).

4 As Sunday stands in relation to the week, so the Fifty Days stand in relation to the year. Sunday is sometimes referred to as the "eighth day," the day of the new creation. So the Easter season serves as an extended period of celebration of the new beginning of things inaugurated in Christ's death and rising.

describes as "the three holy days ... within which [Christ] suffered, lay in the tomb, and arose; the three days of which he said: 'Destroy this temple and in three days I will raise it up.'"[5] Augustine calls the *Triduum* "the three sacred days of his crucifixion, burial and resurrection."[6] Leo the Great sees the events celebrated during the *Triduum* as embracing the whole mystery of redemption. The fact that "Jesus Christ was crucified, died and was buried," he declares, "was not the doom necessary to his own condition, but the method of his redeeming us from captivity." Thus "if we unhesitatingly believe with the heart what we profess with the mouth, in Christ we are crucified, we are dead, we are buried; on the very third day we, too, are raised."[7]

Patristic authors designated these three days as the *Pasch* — a term that is one of triumph, not of sorrow. Its use encompassed *both* the Passion of Christ *and* his passage from death to life. It also included our solidarity with him through faith and baptism. The *Triduum* was seen as a single feast of redemption in which an individual event made sense only as a part of the whole.

Within that *Triduum* the patristic authors saw no sense in the notion that one day was for sorrow and another for joy. It was only as a whole that these three days achieved their end — victory over death. Even the term *Passion*, which later ages came to see as negative, was infused with a sense of triumph. Thus Cyprian could write that "at the sixth hour the Lord was crucified and at

---

[5] *Epistle* 23, 13. St. Ambrose of Milan (*c.* 339-97) is traditionally considered one of the four great Doctors or Teachers of the Western church.

[6] *Epistle* 55, 15, 24. St. Augustine of Hippo (354-430), bishop and one of the Doctors of the church, exercised enormous influence on Western theology due to his massive intellect and deep spirituality.

[7] *Sermon* 72, 3. St. Leo the Great (d. 461), Bishop of Rome, is another of the significant Doctors of the church.

the ninth he washed our sin in his blood that we might be redeemed and have new life. Thus the victory of his Passion was fulfilled."[8]

This integrity or unity of the *Triduum* is sometimes difficult for us to appreciate, because we have become accustomed to seeing the events of Holy Week as independent, each bearing a significance apart from the other events. This, in part, is a product of the rise of humanism during the Renaissance, when Christian piety began to identify with the sufferings of Christ, often dwelling on them to the exclusion of the resurrection, which was their vindication. Much of the Lenten hymnody we have inherited (particularly that of the Pietists[9] as well as that of the last century) reflects this attitude to the cross. The emphasis on sadness, however, is quite alien to the original spirit of the *Triduum*. In the light of our new-found knowledge concerning the beginnings of the observance of the Christian *Pasch*, we must pose some hard questions about later developments.

It is perhaps useful to begin by reminding ourselves that no New Testament author regretted the death of Christ. To be sure, the New Testament presents us with the horror of Christ being subject to the humiliating death of a criminal, but we are never led to wish that the crucifixion had not taken place. Without it we would still be counted as dead.

---

8 *On the Lord's Prayer* 34. St. Cyprian, Bishop of Carthage in North Africa and martyr (d. 258).

9 The Pietists were members of a religious reform movement of the German Lutheran church in the 17th century. They attempted, through devotional meetings with prayer, Bible reading and the like, to infuse a mystical dimension into the lifeless dogmatic orthodoxy of their day. The English translation of Paul Gerhardt's (d. 1676) "O sacred head, sore wounded" is an excellent example of Pietist hymnody.

The crucifixion, as the Fourth Gospel would have it, is Jesus' moment of victory. Jesus reigns from the cross. "When I am lifted up [on the cross] I will draw all to myself" (John 12:32). John presents the often-forgotten *soteriology*, or doctrine of salvation, that merely gazing on the cross was in itself a saving act. For the fourth evangelist the loss of life and the gift of new life are a single reality, not separable chronologically. The grain of wheat that, only in dying, bears a rich harvest (John 12:24) is an interpretive gloss on Jesus' designation of his death on the cross as the hour for the glorification of the Son of Man (John 12:23).

The Christians of the patristic era prepared for the *Pasch* with a short intense fast (from one to six days), often justified by citing the text: "Can the wedding guests fast while the bridegroom is with them? As long as they have the bridegroom with them, they cannot fast. The days will come, when the bridegroom is taken away from them, and then they will fast in that day" (Mark 2:19–20).

This Paschal fast was understood as an act of solidarity between the Christian community and those who had undergone the long period of preparation for baptism (a custom dating back to the first century and witnessed to in the *Didache* [7:46]). In a blending of traditional imagery, the fast marks the bridegroom's departure through death and burial, and quickens the intense longing for his promised return. This longing receives corporate expression in the Paschal Vigil, and finds fulfillment in the sacraments of baptism and eucharist when the church encounters the risen Lord who establishes his presence sacramentally in the church. The fast, then, is entirely oriented toward participation in the Paschal sacraments, and is broken only when the faithful and newly baptized together partake of the spiritual food given them by the Risen One as communion in his eschatological reign.

Prior to the Council of Nicaea, no record exists of a forty-day fast before Easter. Within a few years of the council, however, a forty-day fast was considered such a well-established custom that those churches not yet observing it were being pushed into doing so.[10] The purpose and character of this forty-day period of unbroken ascetical exercises were entirely derived from the festival for which they prepared — the *Pasch*. The *Pasch* is not only an annual celebration of the Passion of Christ but is, for Christians, the yearly reminder of their own incorporation into the Paschal event through baptism. From this perspective, the forty days were seen as a particular time of grace, a period for the faithful to renew their commitment to live the new life of Christ, summoning the tepid to amendment and the fervent to greater progress. Thus, in one Lenten homily, Leo the Great suggests that

> For though there are no seasons which are not full of Divine blessings, and though access is ever open to us to God's mercy through grace, yet now all minds should be moved with greater zeal to spiritual progress and animated by larger confidence when the return of the day on which we were redeemed invites us to the duties of godliness: that we may keep the super-excellent mystery of the Lord's Passion with bodies and hearts purified.[11]

Lent thus has a two-fold character. The first is reparative and restorative: we are re-called to the Paschal mystery into which we were baptized, and set back on the way of Christ from which we have all strayed. With particular force we hear Augustine's words:

---

[10] The exact origin of the forty days remains a matter of debate among scholars. A most convincing case has been made by Thomas Talley (see footnote 3) who suggests that there was a fusion of the forty-day fast observed by the Egyptian church beginning the day after the Epiphany (which was observed as the Baptism of the Lord), imitating Jesus' fast in the wilderness after his baptism and the shorter paschal fast whose origins were quite distinct. In the end, the fast emulating Jesus' fast in the wilderness became detached from the Epiphany and attached to the paschal fast.

[11] Sermon 30.

"Behold who you are: become what you see." The second character of Lent is supportive: we are encouraged to enter more deeply into the mystery of the new life in Christ which, in turn, calls us into solidarity with the poor and marginalized of our society.

An extract from a Lenten sermon of Peter Chrysologus, Bishop of Ravenna from 425 to 450, gives us some insight into the tension between the interior and external dimensions involved in keeping Lent.

> There are three things, my brothers and sisters, which cause faith to stand firm, devotion remain constant, and virtue endure. They are prayer, fasting and mercy [works of love]. Prayer knocks at the door, fasting obtains, mercy receives. Prayer, mercy and fasting: these three are one and they give life to each other.
>
> Fasting is the soul of prayer, mercy is the lifeblood of fasting. Let no one try to separate them; they cannot be separated. If you have only one of them or not all together, you have nothing. So if you pray, fast; if you fast, show mercy; if you want your petition to be heard, hear the petition of others. If you do not close your ear to others you open God's ear to yourself.
>
> When you fast, see the fasting of others. If you want God to know that you are hungry, know that another is hungry. If you hope for mercy, show mercy. If you look for kindness, show kindness. If you want to receive, give. If you ask for yourself what you deny to others, your asking is a mockery.
>
> Let this be the pattern for all when they practice mercy: show mercy to others in the same way, with the same generosity, with the same promptness, as you want others to show mercy to you.
>
> When you fast, if your mercy is thin your harvest will be thin; when you fast, what you pour out in mercy overflows into your barn. Therefore, do not loose by saving, but gather by scattering. Give to the poor, and you give to yourself. You will not be allowed to keep what you have refused to give to others.[12]

---

[12] Sermon 43.

In another Lenten sermon, Leo the Great links the works of love to the faithful observance of Lent.

> If God is love, charity should know no limit, for God cannot be confined.
>
> Any time is the right time for the works of love, but these days of Lent provide a special encouragement. Those who want to be present at the Lord's Passover in holiness of mind and body should seek above all to win this grace, for charity contains all other virtues and covers a multitude of sins.
>
> As we prepare to celebrate that greatest of all mysteries, by which the blood of Jesus Christ did away with our sins, let us first make ready the sacrificial offerings of works of love. In this way we shall give to those who have sinned against us what God in his goodness has already given to us.
>
> Let us now extend to the poor and those afflicted in different ways a more open-handed generosity, so that God may be thanked through many voices and the relief of the needy supported by our fasting. No act of devotion on behalf of the faithful gives God more pleasure than that which is lavished on the poor ... In these acts of giving do not fear a lack of means. A generous spirit is itself great wealth. There can be no shortage of material for generosity where it is Christ who feeds and Christ who is fed. In all this activity there is present the hand of the one who multiplies the bread by breaking it, and increases it by giving it away.[13]

Lent, then, becomes a call to the church to become truly herself. The Christian community is called to surrender itself on all fronts to the grace of the coming *Pasch*, thereby living and exemplifying already the very mystery it is preparing to celebrate.

In this light, the Lenten fast takes on a corporate rather than an individual meaning, for it concentrates the total life of faith into a single act capable of corporate and public performance. For the great teachers of the fourth and fifth centuries, fasting was an act that remained rooted in the reality from which it springs and toward which it points, namely, the fullness of ecclesial life. To

---

13 Sermon 10 in Quadragesima, 3–5.

absolutize the fast and acts of abstinence would be to void them of their power and significance. The meaning and value of the fast, derived from its being the symbol of all the church is, and ought to be, that of a body emptied of any pretension to self-subsistence and filled instead with the gift and presence of Christ who is the church's life, a gift that must continually be given both for us and for the life of the world.

Dissolution

In the fifth century, Lent began to take on a character quite different from that of its origins. This "new" Lent was to dominate the life of the Western churches until the reform of the liturgical year and lectionary, a reform that has been underway during only the past several decades. As we reflect on the practice of this new Lent, readers may well recognize many of the features they associate with the Lents they grew up with, as well as many of the qualities that may persist just under the surface of many parish observances of Lent today, despite efforts to renew this dimension of the church's corporate life.

A variety of factors coalesced to dissolve the symbiotic relationship between prayer, fasting, and mercy, which had been the life blood of the church's observance of Lent. With the legalization of the church by Constantine in 313, and the growing establishment of Christianity as the official religion of the empire, baptism ceased to be a matter for young and old alike, as infant baptism became increasingly the norm. The sense of solidarity once possible in a shared fast with adults, whose fasting was a part of a final stage of preparation for baptism at the Easter Vigil, was no longer possible. At the same time, the practice of public (or canonical) penance, which acknowledged the effects of sin on both the individual and the whole community, fell into disuse. Previously the faithful who were preparing for their reconciliation on Maundy Thursday had fasted in solidarity with those who were set apart as penitents. Now, one more occasion for a corporate manifestation of the ecclesial life through fasting disappeared. Penitents and adult candidates for baptism no longer provided an annual focus for the corporate and Paschal focus of Lent. The effects of this development on the style of Lenten observance was monumental.

The great missionary efforts of the church were also to have a significant effect on the devolution of Lenten practices. For, while many nations and peoples were baptized out of solidarity with their leader who had become Christian, there was little liturgical catechesis that instilled a corporate sense of Lent. Images to explain the Passion began to change. The glue that held the three days of Good Friday, Holy Saturday, and Easter together became unstuck. An increasingly feudal society came to see Good Friday as the day of suffering and Sunday as the day of resurrection, in opposition to the earlier view that also saw Friday as the day when Christ reigned from the cross.

Without the presence in the community of adult candidates for baptism (who were seen to exhibit the effects of their own journey from death to resurrection) or penitents (whose "tears of penitence," as Leo said, "were a second baptism"), and in conjunction with the loss of the Johannine sense of the cross as the instrument of triumph rather than shame, the whole character of Lent began to change.

The sense of the *Triduum*, as the long journey from death to resurrection, celebrated as a single reality, disappeared. The use of the term *Pasch* came to be restricted to the resurrection alone, and its celebration to Easter Day. Easter now stood on its own outside the *Triduum*. The *Triduum* was "recalculated" to become Maundy Thursday, Good Friday, and Holy Saturday (a *Triduum* of death). In time, this was balanced by the creation of a new *Triduum* of Easter Day and the Monday and Tuesday of Easter Week (a *Triduum* of life).[14] No longer considered the *Pasch*, the new *Triduum* came to be considered the last three days of Lent.

---

14 These opposing systems of "three days" remain (probably unintentionally) in *The Book of Common Prayer* (1962), which, like its predecessors, provides propers for Monday and Tuesday in Easter Week alone, pp. 185-190.

With adult candidates for baptism no longer present, the Paschal fast became indistinguishable from the Lenten discipline, and the two merged. At the same time, Eastertide lost its integrity as the week of weeks (the Great Fifty Days), in which the church kept unbroken feast, and became a series of quasi-independent feasts.

In the eighth and ninth centuries, the shape of Lent received its final determination. In the West, Sunday, the day of the Resurrection, could not be a fast day. As a result, some uncertainty arose about when the forty-day fast was to begin. In popular practice, the fast began on Wednesday in Quinquagesima week. Officially, however, Lent began on the following Sunday.

The solution lay in the combination of old and new practices. In the days of canonical penance, individuals were admitted to the state of penitence in a public rite that, among other ceremonies, involved the imposition of ashes as an outward sign of penitence. While the rite remained in the liturgical texts, its practice lapsed. The widespread popular acceptance of the new "tariff penance,"[15] with its recourse to frequent confession and absolution, introduced a new possibility into the shape of Lent. What better way to begin the forty-day fast than with a day when all the faithful could confess their sins and receive ashes as a sign of their solidarity in Adam's sin and death? Ash Wednesday thus emerged at the head of Lent. With the loss of adult candidates for baptism and the end of canonical penance, the Ash Wednesday rite served to tip the balance, and the season became weighed down by penance and

---

[15] The history of the reconciliation of penitents is a long and complex one. The new system developed through the influence of Celtic or Anglo-Saxon missionaries. Confession of sin was secret. Private penances were imposed according to guidelines for confessors in penitential manuals. A penance was intended, first of all, as a punishment. It was also seen as medicinal, helping the sinner to eradicate the qualities that led to the sin in the first place. Over time the penance became fairly light and formal.

fast. The social and Paschal dimensions of Lent were thoroughly dissolved.

In the new Ash Wednesday rite, which cobbled together rites of two distinct and incompatible theologies, the *lex orandi* ceased to provide the Western church with a Lent that balanced the intimately related dynamics of restoration and renewal, interior reparation and external support. The primary emphasis of the new rite was instead interior and restorative alone. It is this Lent that survived until the present reforms.

Lent Today: Reform and Renewal

The initial efforts to reform the celebration of the *Triduum* in the Western church were published under Pius XII in 1955. Of these reforms, perhaps the most influential in its effect was the reform of the Easter Vigil. Not only was the Vigil restored to Holy Saturday night from Saturday morning where it had come to be celebrated, but the new text brought together the richest liturgical diet of the entire church year. It was probably this reform, more than any other, that captured the imaginations of some Anglican parishes and encouraged them, on an unofficial basis, to integrate this most splendid of all liturgies into their own liturgical life.

Because it did not replace anything, the Easter Vigil could be considered on its own merits, and slowly it became the focus for many parish celebrations of the *Pasch*. Gradually there also arose an interest in the other rites of the *Triduum* and, in turn, those of Lent. Liturgists who worked on the new texts for Ash Wednesday and the *Triduum* in *The Book of Alternative Services* had first been won over to the pastoral implications of a renewed Lent by their experiences of the celebration of the Vigil.

The rites in the *BAS* are part of a second stage of the reform of Lent, the *Triduum*, and Eastertide. Inspired, to a large degree, by the reformed rites that were published after the Second Vatican Council, the *BAS* rites can also claim parentage through the work of the ecumenical Joint Liturgical Group of Great Britain, the

Episcopal *Book of Common Prayer* (1979), and even the American United Methodist publication *From Ashes to Fire.*[16] Together these make up a large family of rites based on some common principles for the reform and renewal of the liturgical time between Ash Wednesday and Pentecost. It is most likely that the "parent" traditions would see their rites as works in progress rather than as the "final word."

The first principle behind the reformed texts of the *BAS* is the broader principle lying behind the reform of the whole Calendar, namely, the primacy of the celebration of the Paschal mystery.

> The liturgy of the church celebrates but one mystery: the life, death, and resurrection of Jesus Christ.
>
> Each Sunday is the weekly commemoration of that mystery of Christ. Christians gather each Sunday to celebrate, in word and sacrament, their participation in Christ. The Lord's Day is consequently given primacy over other commemorations.
>
> Each year the weekly commemoration is celebrated with particular joy when the church keeps Passover or Easter. This observance includes forty days of preparation in Lent and fifty days of celebration in the Easter season. Easter is the central festival of the church Year. (p. 14)

The Calendar begins by defining Sunday as the weekly celebration of the Paschal mystery and Easter as its annual commemoration. From that central locus two periods are defined: a season of preparation (Lent) and one of celebration (Easter). The season of Lent now clearly begins on Ash Wednesday without any "warm up," the pre-Lenten Sundays having been integrated into the Epiphany season. Passiontide no longer exists as a distinct season. Its first half is now the Fifth Week of Lent; its second, Holy

---

16 *From Ashes to Fire: Services of Worship for the Seasons of Lent and Easter* (Nashville: Abingdon Press, 1979).

Week. Holy Week begins with the Sunday of the Passion, Palm Sunday, and ends on Holy Saturday. The integrity of the Great Fifty Days is restored as a single uninterrupted season. Ascensiontide is no longer a distinct season, nor is Pentecost treated as an isolated feast with an octave of its own.

While Rogation Days are permitted (Days of Optional Observance, p. 18) they are to be appointed at the time crops are planted. These dates will naturally vary with the wide range of climates across the country. Those who prepared the *BAS* calendar hoped that Rogation Days would not be interpolated into the Easter Season, because their penitential character is inappropriate during this period of celebration. At the very least, if the Rogation Days fall within the Easter season, the liturgical colour should remain that of Easter and not change to purple.

The second principle behind the reform is that Lent is a journey to Easter and not a forty-day meditation on the cross. The journey is corporate and has social implications. This reform intentionally restores the original theology of Lent, the time when the church is called to be its true self in the light of the approaching celebration of the *Pasch*. Lenten activities are corporate in nature and lead us to renew our common life in the Paschal mystery. This renewal, as is obvious from the vows made at every baptism and again at the Easter Vigil, has explicit social implications (pp. 159, 331–32). The Ash Wednesday bidding puts this succinctly.

> Dear friends in Christ,
> every year at the time of the Christian Passover
> we celebrate our redemption
> through the death and resurrection
> of our Lord Jesus Christ.
> Lent is a time to prepare for this celebration
> and to renew our life in the Paschal mystery.

Later in the bidding, the faithful are invited to observe the carefully balanced interior and external dimensions of classical Lenten piety.

I invite you therefore, in the name of the Lord,
to observe a holy Lent
by self-examination, penitence, prayer,
fasting and almsgiving ....
(pp. 282–83)

The Paschal and social dimensions central to Lent, both in origin and as restored, are made explicit in the first eucharistic preface for the season.

Blessed are you, gracious God,
creator of heaven and earth,
because you bid your faithful people
to cleanse their hearts
and to prepare with joy for the paschal feast;
that reborn through the waters of baptism
and renewed in the eucharistic mystery,
we may be more fervent in prayer
and more generous in the works of love.
(p. 230 cf. p. 253)

It would be unfair to suggest that *The Book of Common Prayer* itself was responsible for the general custom of celebrating Lent as a meditation on the crucified Lord. The antiquity of many of its Sunday lections and collects antedates the advent of this particular Lenten piety. It is the larger liturgical context in which the *BCP* was used, however, that nurtured and perpetuated a piety in which the crucifixion and death of Christ overshadowed God's mighty act of resurrection.

A quick glance at any hymn book in general use in the Anglican Church of Canada will illustrate the point. Largely through the way we have chosen our hymnody, we have nurtured a piety in which the crucifixion is the primary focus for Lent. Not surprisingly, vestments, frontals, and hangings decorated with crowns of thorns, nails, spears, and other instruments of the Passion — objects that have found their way into most of our parishes — continue to proclaim visually that the primary focus of Lent is the Passion.

The third principle underlying the reform of Lent in the *BAS* is its presentation of a more balanced and biblical theology of the cross. Lent is not a downhill slide to the greatest defeat in Christian history, followed three days later by a happy ending. While there is no attempt to make light of the horror of the cross, the liturgical texts present it as the instrument through which our salvation is won. As in the Fourth Gospel, the cross is an instrument of victory, not defeat. This depiction of the cross is presented quite consistently in the *BAS* texts, and can be illustrated by a number of examples.

> Most merciful God,
> by the death and resurrection
> of your Son Jesus Christ,
> you created humanity anew.
> May the power of his victorious cross
> transform those who turn in faith
> to him who lives and reigns with you
> and the Holy Spirit,
> one God, now and for ever.
> (Collect, Fifth Sunday in Lent; p. 295)

This view of the cross is found in both eucharistic prefaces provided for use during Holy Week. In the first,

> Blessed are you, gracious God,
> creator of heaven and earth;
> we give you thanks and praise
> through Jesus Christ our Lord,
> who for our sins was lifted high upon the cross,
> that he might draw the whole world to himself.
> By his suffering and death,
> he became the source of eternal salvation
> for all who put their trust in him.
> Therefore with all the host of heaven
> who gather around your throne and the Lamb,
> we raise our voices
> to proclaim the glory of your name.

And in the second,
We give you thanks and praise
through Jesus Christ our Lord,
who for our salvation became obedient unto death.
The tree of defeat became the tree of victory:
where life was lost, life has been restored.
Therefore ...
(p. 221)

The *BAS* liturgy for Good Friday (formerly often depicted as a day of defeat, or observed by a series of sentimental sermons on Christ's last words) is now clearly cast in the Johannine mould. The liturgy itself is entitled "The Celebration of the Lord's Passion" and this tenor is sustained throughout the rite. The part of the liturgy called the "Meditation on the Cross" presents the texts of anthems to be sung in praise of an instrument that won our life. The rubrics following direct that the hymn "Sing my tongue, the glorious battle" or "some other hymn extolling the glory of the cross" is to be sung (p. 317).

The implications of this presentation of the cross are numerous. How we view the cross will affect not only our choice of hymnody but also our preaching and the art that decorates our churches, as well as our choice of those para-liturgical devotions that run the gamut from choral presentations of Stainer's *Crucifixion* or the Pergolesi *Stabat Mater* to Stations of the Cross.

The fourth principle underlying the reform of Lent is the assumption that Easter is the time, above all others, for the celebration of baptism. This timing expresses those principles underlying the many reforms that have taken place in the practice and discipline surrounding Christian initiation within Anglicanism over the past quarter-century. While these cannot be dealt with at length here,[17] they presume, in part, that preparation for baptism is an activity involving the whole community, that it takes place

---

17 Perhaps the easiest summary of these directions is to be found in David R. Holeton ed., *Growing in Newness of Life: Christian Initiation in Anglicanism Today — Papers from the Fourth International Anglican Liturgical Consultation* (Toronto: Anglican Book Centre, 1993).

over an extended period of time in the context of the *catechumenate*,[18] and that there will be adult candidates for baptism, as well as infants and small children.

Today, the increasing number of adult candidates for baptism is helping Anglican communities to discover often neglected or forgotten dimensions of the Christian life. The presence in our midst of adults who are coming to the faith, and learning the Christian life-style, is a gift from God that can help us to face honestly the disparity between the faith we proclaim and the faith enacted in our daily lives. We cannot bring others to faith without becoming aware of the dimension of faithlessness in ourselves. The preparation of others for baptism calls us to a heightened fidelity to the Lord in whom we are dead, buried, and raised.

At the same time, we are discovering that the presence of adults seeking baptism helps us to see the relationship between what Peter Chrysologus and his contemporaries called prayer and mercy. Those who come seeking membership in the Christian community often do so with a clearly formed social conscience and a passion for social justice. They often come to the church because they have heard public church statements on justice issues, and they hope to find a community of faith with a similar passion for justice and peace. Here, again, we are re-called to be faithful to the social implications of our own incorporation in the Paschal mystery.

Just as the readings and ceremonies of the Easter Vigil help to exegete the meaning of the baptisms that take place within its context, so too the presence of baptismal candidates — particularly adults — within parish communities help exegete the Sunday readings for Lent. This is especially true during "Year A," when we read the ancient Johannine *pericopes*, or passages, about Jesus and the Samaritan woman, the raising of Lazarus, and the story of the man born blind (each of which was closely associated with the preparation of candidates for baptism in the church's ancient

---

18 See John W.B. Hill, *Making Disciples — Serving Those Who Are Entering the Christian Life* (Toronto: Hoskin books on Worship and Mission, 1991).

liturgies), but the Lenten lections for all three years were chosen assuming that there would be candidates to be baptized at Easter.

The supportive character of Lent, so prominent in the origins of the season, has been restored. Part of the Lenten discipline — particularly the Paschal fast — is once again in solidarity with those who are going through the last stages of preparation for baptism. The readings describing Jesus as the water who quenches all thirst, and the one who raises Lazarus and gives "true sight," will take on new meaning when heard in the presence of those who will soon have their thirst quenched in baptism and where, in Christ, they will be given a new vision as they are raised to new life from the watery death of the font. The community will see what Jesus promised coming true before their own eyes in the lives of the baptismal candidates just as, at one time, the promises were made true in their own lives through baptism. Without candidates for baptism (particularly adults) within our communities, the lections end up being "heard" with only half the senses. The reinstated baptismal character of Lent highlights the restorative character of the season in which we are all called "to behold what we are and to become what we see."

Pastoral Implications

It is evident that these changes of principle are more than just a series of calendrical adjustments or minor shifts of emphasis. Lent, as presented in the *BAS*, can be understood and appropriately celebrated only when it is acknowledged to represent a major reform of theological emphasis, which has significant implications for the character of the season and its formative effect on the spirituality and piety of the faithful.

In renewing the celebration of Lent and the *Pasch*, it is important not to trivialize customs of the past but to build on them. The Lenten customs of the faithful are rarely the product of spontaneous inventiveness. They are usually a response to teaching delivered by the clergy based on their understanding of the theology of the season and the liturgical texts. The renewal of our celebration of Lent and the *Pasch* requires the same level of confidence in the church and the liturgy as was evident in the practices we inherited. Here, patience and teaching are essential.

In the renewal of Lent, penance and fasting assume a new perspective. We are urged to become aware of how far "off-the-mark" we may be, in both our personal and social lives. Individual penance is the natural response, but the new liturgical texts are particularly helpful in preserving a balance between the personal and corporate dimensions of sin. At the same time, we see the formative character of liturgical texts at their best. The liturgy holds before us a vision of society and human interaction as we believe God would have it. By repeatedly praying the texts, we hope to find ourselves conforming to that vision, as well as being confronted by a sense of divine judgement when we fall short.

Fasting and abstinence are once again finding their place in a surprising variety of Christian traditions, including our own. The dynamic for this new appreciation of their value seems two-fold: one originates in the rediscovery of the direct relationship between fasting and the spiritual journey; the other derives from a sense of solidarity with the disadvantaged and undernourished, when we in North America eat too well. Both motives are quite in keeping with the new orientation of Lent: the former invigorates our quest to conform our lives to Christ; the latter recalls the faithful to the social implications of Christian life (particularly if food not eaten or money not spent on uneaten meals or expensive foods is given to the local food bank or an agency like the Primate's World Relief and Development Fund). Prayer, fasting, and mercy are kept together in healthy tension. There is also a prophetic character to the Lenten fast. By adjusting both the quality and content of our Lenten diet, we signal to those around us that our general dietary habits must change if our planet is to survive.

Care must be taken with the symbols and signs used during the season. Renewing their use involves both long- and short-term goals. Parishes have often been given Lenten vestments and hangings embroidered with symbols of the Passion. While these may be appropriate for the last days of Lent, they are inappropriate during the entirety of the Lenten season. As these vestments are often costly and have considerable associative value, great care, patience, and instruction are needed before a transition can be made to vestments and hangings more in keeping with the restored meaning of Lent and the *Triduum*.

Other areas can be addressed more quickly. One is the practice of veiling certain symbolic objects during Lent. In the high middle ages, objects portraying the victory of the resurrection were hidden from view, so that the attention of the faithful could be directed toward the agony of the cross. In time, the practice was extended so that all images, including those of Christ dying on the cross, were hidden from view. The doors of triptychs were closed, statues were hidden under cloth sacks, and crucifixes were veiled. The average Anglican parish usually has few images other than the cross and painted glass windows (which, fortunately, have never been subject to veiling). Serious questions should be raised as to whether the practice of veiling images is congruent with the reformed theology of Lent as found in the *BAS*. The rubrics intentionally make no mention of veiling the cross when it is brought in on Good Friday (p. 313). It is assumed that the cross will be veiled neither then nor at other times during Lent or Holy Week.

If a parish feels that it needs a richer diet of Lenten symbols, consideration could be given to suggestions made in *From Ashes to Easter*,[19] where the symbols relate to the lectionary and conform to the spirit of the renewed theology of the season.

The character or "tone" we give to our Lenten celebrations is, then, of no small significance. In this, our choice of hymnody plays a major role. Very different statements are made about the nature of the season when we begin by singing "The glory of these forty days/we celebrate with songs of praise" rather than "Forty

---

19 *From Ashes to Easter: Lenten Renewal for the Churches* (Washington D.C.: The Liturgical Conference: Washington, 1979).

days and forty nights." Hymns to Christ on the cross ("O sacred head," "Drop, drop, slow tears," etc.), while often set to music above the general standard, have no place in the liturgy before Good Friday, and even then, their place is doubtful when set against the theology of the cross presented by the liturgy. The power of hymnody can never be underestimated in the formation or renewal of our spirituality.

Until these new patterns become well established in the life of our parishes and in the piety of the faithful, the planning and celebration of the liturgies of Lent and Easter are matters for particular care. We do not serve the People of God well if we simply muddle along using the reformed Lenten texts as a veneer on a traditional Lenten piety accepted uncritically. This serves only to obscure or undermine the reformed character of the new texts, and to create a disturbing tension between the text and piety.

Conclusion

The renewal of the celebration of the liturgical year is an ongoing issue for the whole church. There are still concerns that need to be addressed in the reform of the seasons of Lent and Easter.

The primary reform is the restoration of the *Triduum* to its original shape: Good Friday, Holy Saturday, and Easter. The recovery of a broader sense of the *Pasch* as "the three sacred days of Christ's crucifixion, burial and resurrection" would restore a healthy balance of understanding to a widespread piety that sees the cross and the resurrection as almost irreconcilable opposites.

As parishes work on the renewal of their liturgical celebrations of Lent and the *Pasch*, some of the questions that at present seem only theoretical will begin to emerge as pastoral. The seeds of change are in the reformed liturgical texts with which we live. That they should raise lively questions would be a healthy sign of the dynamic relationship between the *lex orandi* and the *lex credendi*.

LITURGIES OF THE LENTEN SEASON

Ash Wednesday

How great your patience is, O Lord! You are full of compassion and gracious, slow to anger, abounding in mercy, and true! You make your sun rise on the good and on the wicked alike; you send rain on the just and the unjust alike. You do not desire the death of sinners; you would rather that they turn away from wickedness and truly live. By your patience you lead us to repentance, although many people by reason of hardened hearts and stubborn wills are storing up wrath in themselves for the day of wrath and of the revealing of your righteous judgement. You will judge all people according to their works. You are the one who will forget our transgressions when we turn from our wickedness to your mercy and truth. Grant to us through our ministry, by which you have refuted all sorts of dreadful errors, and by which many have already been liberated, that still many more may be liberated. Whether it is through the sacrament of your holy baptism, or through the sacrifice of a broken spirit and a contrite and humbled heart, or through the sorrow of repentance, may still many more people deserve to receive forgiveness of their sins and blasphemies. There is no help at all, except in your matchless compassion and strength, in the truth of your baptism, and in the keys of the kingdom of heaven in your holy church. We must not despair of people as long as they live on this earth through your patience … when we see that, at last, corrected by you, they flee to your matchless goodness and prefer the heavenly and eternal life to come to all the lures of the life of this world.

St. Augustine, *Concerning the Nature of God*, 48

COLOUR: PURPLE OR LENTEN ARRAY[20]

The Lenten propers of the *BAS* give renewed attention to the baptismal aspect of the Paschal celebration. Year A in particular gathers texts and prayers which treat of baptismal themes.

The rite for Ash Wednesday emphasizes the penitential character of the Lenten season, although the instruction (p. 281) after the (optional) sermon refers to renewal "in the Paschal mystery." Penitence, then, is seen as a deepening of Christian life already begun in baptism.

Preparation for Ash Wednesday requires some consideration of what kind of balance must be struck in a particular setting between spoken word and song, since the service can be among the wordiest of the year.

ITEMS NEEDED FOR THE SERVICE

- altar vested in purple or Lenten Array
- purple chasuble, or purple stole (or of Lenten Array)
- sacramentary
- ashes
- a bowl of water, with soap and a towel for the presider to wash his or her hands after imposing ashes
- [processional cross, torches, incense]
- [sufficient bread and wine]

THE GATHERING OF THE COMMUNITY

The rubrics for the rite are clear that the liturgy on this day is to begin quite starkly, without announcement or hymn, but with a simple greeting and prayer (p. 281). The presiding celebrant (and other ministers) enter(s) and reverence(s) the altar [and the

---

[20] Used in some places as an alternative to purple, the Lenten Array is generally an unbleached cotton, often with banding of black and deep red. Its plainness, reminiscent of sackcloth, is intended to highlight the austerity of the season.

congregation]. Extending the hands, the presider greets the congregation, saying or singing, "The Lord be with you." After the people's response and the invitation to pray, sufficient time needs to be given for people to pray in silence before the collect. Everyone then sits for the readings.

The Proclamation of the Word

Three readings are appointed to be read, along with a psalm between the first two lections. As the Psalter is the primary hymnal of the church, congregations should be encouraged to learn to sing psalms whenever possible, if they do not already do so.[21] ("Alleluia" is not sung at this service, nor throughout Lent.) A procession with cross and torches can help to highlight the proclamation of the Gospel and conduct the gospeller to the customary place of reading. If it is usual at other times of the year to sing an alleluia before the Gospel, perhaps with the sentence of the day, a parish could adopt the practice of singing an alternative acclamation. A traditional text for this acclamation during Lent is "Praise to you, Lord Jesus Christ, King of eternal glory"[22] before the Gospel. Alternatively, another psalm or tract can be sung. Finally, a hymn can be sung that is generally consonant with the theme of the Gospel. (The practice of singing part of the hymn before the Gospel and part of it after the Gospel should be avoided, as it is unfair to both hymn and gospel.) The Gospel is announced in the customary fashion (pp. 188 and 233). A sermon usually follows the Gospel.

While the *BAS* indicates that a sermon is optional on this day, it would be unfortunate to miss this privileged opportunity to invite people to repentance and active participation in the celebration of Lent. A period of silence may follow the sermon, sufficient to allow people time to consider the message.

---

[21] See chapter 6 for resources.

[22] There are many musical settings of this text and its variants.

Penitential Rite

The presider or some other minister addresses the people in the words on p. 281. The entire congregation is then invited to kneel, with the presider kneeling either in the midst of the congregation, in a centre aisle, or on the chancel steps, facing the altar. In order to express unity between people and officiating ministers, it is advisable that everyone face in the same direction.

If they are to be used, ashes in a bowl should be brought into close proximity to the presider. (Ashes are made by burning palms saved from the previous year's Sunday of the Passion. As they produce a rather acrid smoke, they should be burned well before the service in a well-ventilated area. Any fragments can be ground fine with the back of a spoon. A little goes a long way.) While all are kneeling, a generous silence should be kept in order to allow people, called to repentance, to consider their situation. Psalm 51 can be sung by all, sung by a choir or cantor with the congregation singing the refrain, or said by all. Immediately following the psalm, the litany of penitence begins without further announcement. The prayer on page 285 is not a blessing of the ashes; the presider simply prays with the hands in the *orans* position.

Those wishing to receive ashes come forward to kneel or stand either at the chancel steps or at an altar rail. The presider applies the ashes by dipping the thumb into the bowl and tracing a cross on the forehead of each person. (An assisting minister or other member of the congregation may impose ashes on the presider before others receive them.) The phrase, "Remember you are dust, and to dust you shall return," must be committed to memory, as it will not be possible to administer ashes while carrying a book. After everyone has received ashes, the presider goes to the credence table to cleanse his or her hands. The presider again kneels, and the confession concludes in the words on page 285. The presider then stands to give the absolution. People may be invited to stand by means of a gesture, which is preferable to a verbal announcement. The peace is then exchanged.

The Celebration of the Eucharist

The preparation of the gifts can proceed in the accustomed way while a hymn is sung or other music played. If the third eucharistic prayer is to be used, the first of the two Lenten prefaces is probably most appropriate. While there are no directions in the *BAS* for concluding the Ash Wednesday liturgy, simplicity and economy of action would complement the beginning of the service. A hymn, psalm, or refrain could be sung during communion. The proper prayer after communion may be said. The doxology, "Glory to God, whose power working in us ..." might then be omitted throughout the season, in order to provide variety. Following the dismissal, the ministers reverence the altar (and the people) and depart.

A Penitential Order

The Lord is gracious and merciful, preferring the repentance of the sinner to his death, slow to anger and abounding in steadfast love, not being impatient as we are but waiting a whole lifetime for our return to him. He is high above evil or rather he repents of evil, so that if we repent of our sins he repents of his threats and does not carry them out, his heart softening as we change our attitude.

St. Jerome, *On the Book of Joel*

The Penitential Order is found in the *BAS* on pages 216–217. While it may be used at any time of the year, either before the eucharist or as a separate service, it may be also used to begin the eucharist on Sundays during Lent, in order that people have a genuine opportunity to participate in a corporate act of repentance. A variety of instructional materials can help people prepare for this action. Articles in bulletins or newsletters can give direction in examination of conscience. Many Anglicans (not to mention people of various Protestant denominations) are rediscovering the value of individual confession, using one of the forms for the Reconciliation of a Penitent (pp. 167–172). In places where that rite is used, individual penitents might be invited to confess shortly before the Sunday liturgy. The corporate action would then be seen as a complement to the individual action.

The order begins with the presiding celebrant entering and reverencing the altar (and the people). The celebrant uses the apostolic greeting and adds an additional verse, with response. The collect for purity is then said by all.

The *BAS* provides a list of passages of Scripture that may be read. The choice might be determined by the general theme or tenor of the rest of the service on that day. For example, on the

Third Sunday in Lent, Year B, the first reading at the eucharist is Exodus 20:1–17, the Decalogue. The reading at the Penitential Order that day could be Mark 12:28–34, Jesus' summary of the law. The passage chosen may be read by the presider or any other person. A period of silence may follow the reading to allow people time to reflect on the reading and to make connections between it and their own lives.

People are then invited to confession. Kneeling may be the most appropriate posture for people to assume.[23] A generous time of silence could again be kept. Finally, the presider stands and gives the absolution. The service might continue with the singing of the *Kyrie Eleison* or *Trisagion.* The Gloria is not used during Lent. If the *Trisagion* is unfamiliar to the congregation, a musical setting could be selected and used at this point in the service every week during Lent, so that by Good Friday it would be well enough known to be sung during the first anthem in the course of meditating on the cross (pp. 314–316).

The impact of the Penitential Order comes in no small measure from its position at the beginning of the eucharistic liturgy during Lent (as suggested in the *BAS* rubrics). The intention is not to inculcate guilt but repentance. When considering Lent and Easter together, it is possible to emphasize the different foci of the two seasons by the way of beginning. Let Eastertide be significantly different. For example, omit the Collect for Purity, and go directly from the Easter greeting to "Glory to God." Instead of using the confession and absolution (pp. 191 and 239–240), include a penitential intercession in the Prayers of the People. Penitence will thus still be a part of the liturgy, but the emphasis in Eastertide will have moved from *asking* for forgiveness to *celebrating* redemption effected in the Paschal Mystery.

If a further symbolic action is desired for the Penitential Order, a congregation might consider the use of the *asperges*, or

---

23 It should be noted, however, that in Luke 18:11, 13 standing is considered a suitable posture even for the confession of sin.

sprinkling of the people, while verses from Psalm 51 are sung. This is an excellent tactile reminder of the baptismal mystery toward which the whole season points. While the *Kyrie* was not originally penitential in character, it has gained that association through time. A more extended musical setting of this text, perhaps interpolated with penitential petitions, might serve as another means to express the people's repentance.

Holy Week

The Sunday of the Passion with the Liturgy of the Palms

He rode on the ass to give us examples of holy wisdom. It was not just to fulfil prophecies, nor to plant the word of truth. By these events he has given us guidance for our lives, teaching us how to live worthily. When he was born he did not go looking for a big house, nor look for a rich and famous mother, but found a poor woman whose husband was a carpenter. He was born in a stable, and placed in a manger. When he chose his apostles, he did not choose scholars or intellectuals, nor wealthy or upper class people. Instead, he chose poor men, from poor families, unknown to anyone. His bed was straw, his clothing was plain and ordinary. He had no fixed address. When he needed to go anywhere, he went by foot, and got tired travelling. Even here he lays down a standard of measurement. There is no need of the more expensive horse or mule; an ass will suffice. In all things we should confine ourselves to what we need.

And let us think about the prophecy: Behold, your king will come to you, sitting upon an ass, and a colt the foal of her who is used to the yoke. He doesn't come in a chariot as other kings do; he demands no tribute, has no aides or bodyguards. In this too he shows his gentleness …

So let us also do things the apostles and people did. Let us sing out our hymns. Let us give our garments to those who bear him. Others put their cloak onto the ass he rode; still others spread their clothing before his feet. We are not asked to strip off our clothes, just to give a little. Why do we show not even this little sign of zeal when we see him naked?

St. John Chrysostom, Homily 67 on Matthew

Two different forces are at work in defining the liturgical atmosphere of this day, as the name for the Sunday suggests. The Liturgy of the Palms is a triumphant recollection of Jesus' entry into Jerusalem, a celebration of Christ as king. The lectionary readings, on the other hand, focus on the Passion, contrasting the "Hosannas" of the procession with the rejection of Jesus in the call to "crucify him." This duality reflects the joining of two developments from the evolution of Paschal liturgies during the early centuries of the church.

When the celebration of the Christian Passover had become fixed on Saturday night or Sunday, the previous Sunday became the logical day to experience the Passion narratives and the themes we normally associate with Good Friday. This pattern would have provided a reading of the Passion on one Sunday, followed by a period of fasting during the week, and climaxing with the celebration of Easter at the Great Vigil. The introduction of the palm procession into the Passion Sunday liturgy probably originated in Jerusalem from the tendency to historicize details of Jesus' last days and hours. The geographic locations mentioned in the New Testament accounts became the focal points for observing each event in order throughout the week in its prescribed location. The triumphal entry from the Mount of Olives into Jerusalem was re-enacted on the Sunday afternoon beginning the observance of Holy Week.[24] The tradition of Passion Sunday remained normative in much of the Western church for centuries, with the

---

[24] Among the sources we have for the Jerusalem customs is the narrative of the tour taken to the Holy Land by the Spanish nun, Egeria (or "Etheria"), at the end of the fourth century.

palm procession only fully accepted by the tenth or eleventh century, while at the same time, keeping the element of Jesus' Passion.

The Liturgy provided for Passion Sunday in the *BAS* follows Western tradition from the middle ages to the present by accommodating both of these influences. The Liturgy of the Palms, followed by the Passion reading, gives this liturgy a particular movement: the height of triumph descending to the depths of the Passion; the triumphant Messiah understood in the light of the cross.

There are some benefits to this arrangement. First, the triumph of the procession of palms is preserved, while allowing a transition to the more sombre tone of Holy Week. Second, the story of the entry into Jersusalem precedes the Passion, thus permitting two versions of the Passion each year (one from the *synoptics* on Passion Sunday, the other from the Gospel of John on Good Friday). While the Passion narratives bear many similarities to one another, the sermon should not subject them to a false harmonization. Instead, people could be encouraged to notice the differences in tone, emphasis, and understanding of each evangelist. Also, it is important to recognize that many parishioners will be present only for Passion Sunday and Easter Sunday. This arrangement ensures that the central place of the Passion readings is not overlooked.

In order to focus on the two aspects of Passion/Palm Sunday, it may be both possible and appropriate to separate the two parts by using the Passion readings during the morning eucharist, and by celebrating the Liturgy of the Palms later in the day, immediately before evensong or Evening Prayer. While the contrast of the Palm/Passion themes is weakened by doing this, each receives a more singular focus. Similarly, the more complex arrangement of the hybrid liturgy is replaced by two simpler ones. Such an arrangement inverts the order of the events being celebrated for this particular Sunday, but as it stands, the current arrangement already inverts the order of the week by moving from palms to Passion on Sunday, requiring a "rewinding in time" for the pre-Passion events commemorated from Monday through Thursday of Holy Week. If the order of events is of particular concern, a palm procession on Sunday afternoon provides a consistent beginning to the movement of Holy Week from palms to cross to resurrection. Parishioners inclined to attend only the Sunday morning liturgies are then presented with the ancient pattern of hearing the Passion narrative one week and the Easter proclamation the next. While wresting palms from the hands of parishioners on the Sunday morning may seem a daunting task for presiders and worship committees to take on, it is well worth considering.

Colour: Passion Red

The colour should be a deep or blood red. Red vestments or appointments associated with festivals of the Holy Spirit should be of a different hue and would not be used during Holy Week.

Items Needed for the Service

For the Liturgy of the Palms

- a table of reasonable size and dignity on which to set palm branches
- a bucket of holy water and a sprinkler (if it is desired to sprinkle the branches)
- [thurible and incense]
- a book marked at the gospel lection of Jesus' entry into Jerusalem:
  - Year A — Matthew 21:1-11
  - Year B — Mark 11:1–11 or John 12:12–16
  - Year C — Luke 19:28–40
- processional cross
- [torches]

For the Liturgy of the Day

- sacramentary
- Bible or lectionary marked
- if the Passion is read dramatically, booklets containing narrative distributed among readers
- vessels, bread, and wine for the holy communion

THE LITURGY OF THE PALMS

Whether the liturgy of the palms precedes the Sunday eucharist or is incorporated into evensong later in the day, its form as found in the *BAS* can be followed without any adaptation.

The liturgy of the palms is a celebration of Christ as king: the procession mirrors Christ's triumphal entry into Jerusalem. The physical activity of movement and song, in the context of recalling the gospel story, assists us to welcome Christ into our own community and proclaim him as our king. The *BAS* rubrics suggest beginning the liturgy in a location other than the body of the church — for instance, in the church hall or basement — or, weather and location permitting, outside on the lawn, or even in the parking lot. The importance of beginning elsewhere lies in the opportunity to move from somewhere to somewhere else (that is, actually processing). Because the first part of the liturgy includes an introductory exhortation and prayers, it is important to find the best place where the presider can be heard, and where the congregation can gather around. There is provision for a station, or stopping point, on the way back into the church building, at which there will be a prayer, either spoken or sung. If the parking lot is to be used for gathering at the beginning or at some time during the procession, areas may need to be marked off in advance with cones or ropes, to ensure that the congregation is not left standing among the vehicles. As always, liturgical action planned for outdoors should be covered by a back-up plan, in case of rain or snow.

In some cases, because of architecture or weather, the liturgy of the palms may need to be done completely inside the church building. In this case, a "stylized" procession can be planned, but care should be taken to avoid the pretence of a procession that is symbolically bereft. For example, singing (or saying), "Let us go forth in peace," followed by the procession of a few ministers, circling around a smallish church while the congregation remains stationary, may seem rather unreal. In such a setting, if the congregation is small enough or the church big enough, the congregation may gather at the back and then process around the church to the front. Or, if the congregation remains in the pews, the drama of a procession may be enhanced by the participation of members or representatives of various congregational groups — such as the choir, the servers, Sunday school children, and others. In some places, liturgical dance has been used effectively to represent the triumphal entry and welcome of Christ into the parish community.

On special occasions such as this — with unfamiliar movement and activity — sidespeople, servers, and musicians play an important role. Sidespeople need to be ready to direct and assist people to do what is asked of them. The sidespeople will also have to be aware of what happens during the procession, in order to help move people forward. In addition, sidespeople may be called upon to hold doors, redirect parking lot traffic, re-light acolytes' candles on entering the church, and even give signals to the organist if music is to be played when the procession enters the building. All these tasks can and should be anticipated and planned in advance, in order for those doing them to feel confident in fulfilling their roles.

Servers will likewise need to be rehearsed. Someone will need to carry the sacramentary and the Bible or gospel book during the procession. Extra servers may be required, especially if incense is used during the procession. If the procession goes outside, processional torches may need to be re-lit. (Wind-proof torches can be purchased, but a ready pack of matches at the door is generally cheaper.)

During an indoor procession, the musicians can simply use the already existing instruments and resources. If, however, the procession is elaborate or outdoors, extra planning will be required. Depending on the music chosen, instrumentalists may be asked to support congregational singing. A progressive lack of coordination between the front and back of a processing line of congregants seems a normal occurrence. Placing musicians (choir, brass, guitars, etc.) in the middle of a procession can help keep the singing together. On the other hand, anticipating and living with the inevitable lack of coordination is usually the best policy!

If the Liturgy of the Palms is to take place outside of the regular worship space, it is best to provide each member of the congregation with a pamphlet printed with their responses from the *BAS* and the words of all the hymns. This keeps parishioners from having to carry and juggle two different books.

Palm branches can be purchased from any number of church supply houses, and are even available pre-folded into palm crosses. Whether pre-folded or folded at the local church, the use of palm crosses for the procession raises some questions. For example, what does a palm cross symbolize? Is it a visual mixed metaphor? Is it adequate to the task of representing a branch to be waved in a triumphal procession? While there may be some merit in continuing to hand out palm crosses as visual representations of the combined themes of the Passion/Palm Sunday observance, they do not really belong in the palm procession. For processions, regular palm branches can readily be obtained in large sizes adequate to the task at hand.

Given the symbolic nature of the procession in welcoming Christ into our own community, in this place at this time, presiders and worship committees might consider dispensing with palms altogether and replacing them with branches from local trees and shrubs. Members of the congregation may bring their own branches, intensifying their involvement in the liturgical action and connecting the liturgical symbolism to themselves and their own situations.

If the palm procession is incorporated into the celebration of the eucharist, the presider's vestments will be those used for a Passiontide eucharist. If it precedes evensong, cassock, surplus and stole, or hood and scarf may be worn, or a cope if one is available. The colour is still Passion red.

The liturgy begins with the acclamation, "Blessed is he who comes ..." (p. 297). This may be sung as a choir anthem or a solo for a cantor, or used as a greeting with the response, "Hosanna in the highest," from the congregation. The introduction is read, followed by the prayer and the gospel account of the triumphant entry. If the parish has a tradition of gospel processions,[25] the servers and gospeller move to a more central location among or near the congregation with cross and torches.

A blessing for the palms is then said. The blessing prayer provided on page 298 is structured as a eucharistic prayer in which God is blessed for the "acts of love by which [God has] redeemed us." The presider may thus stand in the *orans* position throughout the prayer. The palms are then distributed by the presider and any others, lay or ordained, as may conveniently assist.

This prayer is based on the understanding that the palms, or any object, become blessed through their use in the liturgical celebration. Some parishes adumbrate the blessing prayer by censing the palms and sprinkling holy water on them at the conclusion of the prayer. In this case, prepare the table with the branches, a vessel of water, and a branch or *aspergillum* for sprinkling placed next to them. After the censing and sprinkling, the branches are distributed. As the distribution may take some time, there is opportunity for a psalm, hymn, anthem, or other musical offering. The palms may be distributed to the congregation, or people can be invited to come forward and pick up a palm.

The procession then begins with "Let us go forth in peace ..." Provision is made for a station prayer during the procession, which provides a transition from the theme of triumph to the Passion account. (It also works well when the procession is separated from the morning's Passion emphasis.) The choice of music can be influenced by whether the procession is in the context of the eucharist or evensong. If the liturgy is to continue with the eucharist, hymns which include the Passion theme, such as "Ride on!, ride on," work well. At evensong, the emphasis is somewhat different and may require some adjustment (see the section on evensong, below).

---

25 See David Holeton et al., *Let Us Give Thanks* (Toronto: Hoskin Books, 1991), 19.

Once the procession has come to an end, the liturgy continues either with the eucharist (Sunday morning) or evensong (Sunday evening). When paired with the eucharist, the Liturgy of the Palms is concluded with the Collect of the Day. With evensong several options are possible as discussed below.

The Eucharist on Passion Sunday

The eucharist is celebrated as usual, but begins with the first reading rather than the apostolic greeting. The Passion Gospel may be read in parts by various members of the congregation. This is best done either sung throughout by a few voices or read dramatically by appointed readers. The readers could either move to the front of the church (as is frequently done) or read standing in their places. The latter can help to create a sense in which the whole congregation lives in the middle of the story and participates. It is customary in many churches to have the congregation jointly take the parts that voice the rejection of various parties in the story, such as "Crucify him, crucify him!" While it is appropriate for the faithful to identify with the fallen humanity that rejects Christ, we need to remember that the evangelist's central purpose in recounting the Passion story is to inspire faith, not inflict guilt. The congregation as a whole, then, might be given small parts that are not exclusively negative. The choir or another appointed group of readers could read the crowd passages. Some churches make a habit of having the part of Jesus read by the parish priest. While there is nothing wrong with the clergy taking this part, there is no particular reason why they should.

Whichever way is chosen to recount the Passion narrative, rehearsal is essential. Each reader should be familiar with who is taking the other parts and from where they will be reading. Hearing their own voices from different places in the church building will also prepare participants to read with more understanding and dramatic energy during the liturgy. Although the *BAS* makes no mention of it, the Passion reading on this day is traditionally introduced with the words, "The Passion of our Lord Jesus Christ according to ..."

The creed and confession of sin are normally omitted when the liturgy of the palms takes place.

Evensong

If the palm procession is to be followed by evensong, some care will need to be taken in knitting the two pieces together appropriately and smoothly. Since, at evensong, the Collect of the Day comes after the Prayers of the People and not at the beginning, it cannot be used to make this transition. Further, the collect is meant to continue the movement from palms to Passion, while the readings for evening prayer (p. 462) are not focused on the Passion. The first reading from Zechariah does foreshadow it, but the gospel lections for both years one and two (in Matthew and Luke respectively) are the continuation of the story of the entrance into Jerusalem, including the driving out of the money-changers in the temple. Given this thematic focus, those choosing hymns for the palm procession may wish to avoid moving on to Passion themes right away, by saving hymns such as "Ride on! ride on" for inclusion as an office hymn near the end of the liturgy.

Once the palm procession has concluded and all have returned to their places, the transition to evensong could be accomplished in one of three ways. The most natural way is to have a collect prayer of some sort. The prayer for a station during the procession (p. 299) might serve. Otherwise, one will have to be written in advance. The content of such a prayer would appropriately reflect the triumphal entry into Jerusalem, but also provide a transition to the themes of the evensong. On the other hand, if music is desired to close the palm liturgy, an anthem or hymn could be chosen to begin after everyone is seated. Something short and triumphant in tone would be particularly appropriate. Psalm 103, appointed for that evening, follows. Finally, if people were in their places by the time the last verse or refrain of a processional hymn were sung, the liturgy could continue by going directly to the appointed psalm. In any case, the usual introductory responses for evening prayer are omitted. (Attempting to insert a form of the Service of Light is inadvisable.)

Evensong would then continue as usual, with the possible addition of an office hymn before the dismissal as mentioned above. Planners might wish to consider using canticles such as 22 or 24 (pp. 91 and 93) following the readings.

Monday, Tuesday, and Wednesday in Holy Week

Is there anything which the hearts of the faithful may not promise themselves from the grace of God? It was not enough that the only Son of God, co-eternal with the Father, should be born as a mortal from a mortal for them — he even died for them at human hands, whom he had created. What God promises us for the future is great, but what we recall as already done for us is much greater. When Christ died for the wicked, where were they or what were they? Who can doubt that he will give the saints his life, since he has already given them his death? Why is human weakness slow to believe that we will one day live with God? A much more incredible thing has already happened: God died for human beings.

St. Augustine, Sermon Guelf 3

Colour: Passion Red

While there are no special liturgies besides the eucharist for these days during Holy Week, they have been days of solemn observance in the church from early on. Many churches find they have members willing to make the effort to attend services on these days, despite the busy liturgical schedule the rest of the week.

The proper readings for each day (pp. 301–303) provide some good opportunities for homilies or meditations in preparation for the celebration of the Great Three Days. The Gospel for Monday is the story of the anointing of Jesus' feet by Mary at Bethany as a preparation for his death. Tuesday provides two sections from the Gospel of John dealing with interpretations of Jesus' coming crucifixion: first, as the grain of wheat that falls into the earth and dies in order that it bear much fruit; second, as his "glorification" when he is lifted up so that all may be drawn to him. The Wednesday reading deals with the betrayal by Judas.

The Triduum
The Great Three Days

Maundy Thursday

Love, and do what you will. If you keep silent, do so out of love. If you speak aloud, do so out of love. If you correct, do so out of love. If you spare another, do so out of love. Let the root of love be within. Nothing can spring from this root except what is good.

St. Augustine, On the First Epistle of John 7, 8

Colour: Passion Red or White

See notes below.

Items Needed for the Service

- basin and pitcher; the water should be very warm when poured into the pitcher before the service, in order to be still a pleasant temperature during the washing of feet
- towels
- a visible place for people to sit while their feet are washed; extra chairs as necessary
- bread and wine for the eucharist (including sufficient quantity for communion on Good Friday)
- [if the eucharist is reserved for the next day, a dignified place for the repose of the sacrament (see notes below)]

This day is one of the most complex of Holy Week. It combines the commemoration of the Last Supper (which has given rise to the use of white vestments on this day), the reconciliation of penitents, and various preparatory rites for baptism at the Great Vigil of Easter, in particular the consecration of oils. (In addition, there is the more recent custom of the renewal of priestly vows on this day. It is often said that few lay people come to the latter, but the exclusively clerical nature of such an action would hardly encourage any! A more suitable occasion for such re-affirmation might be a conference of clergy with their bishop.)

While the consecration of oils on Maundy Thursday day has the benefit of being chronologically close to the Vigil, the *BAS* does not, in fact, tie the consecration of oils to any particular occasion. As oils are consecrated by the bishop for an entire diocese, one might ask whether a good representation of its population will be able to attend the cathedral on Maundy Thursday. A diocesan synod might be a more appropriate time for the consecration of oils.

Two sorts of oil are traditionally used in the life of the church. Chrism — olive oil with an admixture of balsam — may be used to sign baptismal candidates with the cross after the water bath. Consecrated oil is used to anoint the sick. To consecrate oil for the sick at a diocesan gathering makes clear that the use of this oil has a decided ecclesial and sacramental dimension, and is not a substance that someone with an independent charism might use.

Regrettably, an element of the day's rite that is still entirely absent from the *BAS* is the reconciliation of penitents. When the church exercised a discipline of penance during its first few centuries, those who had committed grave and public sin still remained in relationship with the church. Although barred from receiving the eucharist, these people were nevertheless on a trajectory toward reconciliation. A service of reconciliation recognized this on Maundy Thursday. (Such a service is attested to by St. Jerome at the beginning of the fifth century, and also by a document, attributed to Pope Silvester, from the last part of the same century.)

A modern attempt to take seriously the reconciliation of those who have been estranged in some way from the church can be found in John Hill's *Making Disciples*.[26] The rites he proposes for

---

[26] John W.B. Hill, *Making Disciples — Serving Those Who Are Entering the Christian Life* (Toronto: Hoskin books on Worship and Mission, 1991).

penitents conclude on Maundy Thursday, the penitents themselves bearing witness to a dimension of discipleship to which we are all are called. In this public rite, there is a recognition of the corporate nature of the church that is wounded by our sins. Still more, there is the tremendous sense of the mercy of God who responds graciously to the prayers of the church.

The *BAS* rite for Maundy Thursday encourages a single celebration, preferably in the evening. Evidence for an evening eucharist is no older than the late fourth century. Nevertheless, the appropriateness of the custom in its evocation of the Last Supper has convinced many today. Also, the evening may be the one time in the day most convenient for the majority of busy people to attend.

Parishes often begin the celebration with a common meal. This should *not* be a "Christian Seder." There is much to be said for efforts to educate Christians about Jewish practice and custom, as well as the Jewish roots of the eucharist and other dimensions of Christianity. Such education should not, however, be a pretext for taking another faith community's rite and, as is often the case, trying to "Christianize" it, to reveal its "true" meaning as understood in Christ. It should go without saying that this is deeply offensive to many Jews. Presumably, Christians would likewise question the validity of a Jewish group "celebrating" the eucharist, without the consultation or involvement of actual Christians.

What is more, the use of a "Seder" on this night skews the forward movement of the church's own rites at this time. The Seder is very much a celebration of "this night" being the night of redemption from bondage in Egypt. For Christians, the great night is the night of the Great Vigil. This focus would be lost through a too early anticipation of it on Maundy Thursday.[27]

---

27 See Kevin Flynn, "Christians and Seder Suppers," *Liturgy Canada*, Epiphany 1991, 9–11.

A distinctive feature of the Maundy Thursday rite in the *BAS* is the washing of feet. In the ancient world, foot washing was a common gesture of courtesy extended to guests. It is in monastic practice, however, that we find the origins of the liturgical rite. Monastic communities began extending the gesture not only to guests but to those poor who came seeking food. The custom eventually became ritualized on the solemn occasion of Maundy Thursday, when the monks thought to imitate the example of Jesus. The abbot or prior would wash the feet of his brethren during the singing of John 13, and various hymns and chants. Among the most lovely of these chants is the haunting *Ubi caritas et amor, Deus ibi est* ("Where there is love and loving kindness, there is God").

The traditional colour for Maundy Thursday is white. This colour distinguishes the day as the beginning of the Lord's Passover. It focuses, too, on the institution of the Lord's Supper. Passion Red, when used this day as during the rest of Holy Week, emphasizes the unity of the week. Planners will have to choose between the two colours.

Throughout the readings, prayers, and actions of the rite, the note of love is sounded: love revealed in Jesus' obedience to the Father, love as his command to his followers, love in the institution of the sacrament. The collect refers to our celebrating "this sign of his great love." The prayer over the gifts asks that all be "bound together in his love"; after communion we pray to God, the "source of all love," that the new commandment[28] be written in our hearts. Love is revealed in the reconciliation of penitents. It is demonstrated in the washing of feet, a visible parable of the eucharist. The presider's exhortation emphasizes the service aspect of the practice. A future revision of this text might include the baptismal dimension as well: "Unless I wash you, you have no part in me."

---

[28] Latin: *mandatum novum*, from which comes the word "Maundy."

In some churches, the Good Friday liturgy concludes with a Meditation on the Cross of Jesus, which reflects the traditionally aliturgical character of this day — a day when the eucharist would not be celebrated and people would not receive communion.[29] The *BAS* also makes provision for the reservation of the sacrament that is distributed on Good Friday. This requires a dignified place of reservation, whether on the altar in a chapel, in an aumbry, or in some other specially prepared place. (Propers are also provided for the celebration of the eucharist on Good Friday.)

The Gathering of the Community

The rite begins with an exhortation by the presider to the congregation, reminding people that the events of the past are fully present now in all their gracious and saving power: "This is the day ..." The rubric indicates that "the eucharist follows in the usual manner." A hymn or other song of praise could be sung, and then comes the collect.

The Proclamation of the Word

Sets of readings are provided for years A, B, and C. Whenever the washing of feet is performed, the readings for year A are used. A further exhortation is supplied, and follows the sermon. As this exhortation refers to Jesus' example in John 13, readings from years B or C could be used in parishes where the foot washing is well known and established. Hearing the narratives of the institution of the eucharist side by side with the washing of feet can shed new light on both.

---

[29] Such was the custom of the papal liturgy of the early middle ages. Titular and presbyteral churches, however, reserved consecrated bread and wine for communion of the faithful on Good Friday.

The Washing of Feet

The *BAS* simply directs that "representative members of the congregation" be invited in advance to have their feet washed. This need not be restricted to twelve men. Any age and number can be appropriate. At relatively small gatherings, the entire congregation might participate. In any event, people need to come prepared. Some may be shy and so need to be encouraged. Women need to remember not to wear panty hose! If the presider wears a chasuble, it is usually a good idea to remove it for the foot washing. Whether the participants are few or many in number, those planning and leading the service need to be comfortable with the fact the washing cannot be done quickly or fastidiously. If a server or other assistant can help with drying, the service will move forward at a good pace. Musical leadership is also crucial. A selection of chants and hymns can assist the congregation's meditation during the washing.

Some people have proposed alternatives to the foot washing that are thought to be modern dynamic equivalents. Among these is the practice of shining the congregation's shoes. While this may have the benefit of emphasizing the aspect of humble service, it cannot evoke the cleansing or baptismal dimensions of which John 13 speaks.

The service continues with the Prayers of the People, followed by the Peace. There is no need to use the general confession (pp. 191 and 239). The liturgy of the next day offers a great deal of scope for self-examination and penitence. Let the greater emphasis fall at that time. On Maundy Thursday the Prayers of the People could contain a penitential petition.

The Celebration of the Eucharist

Eucharistic Prayers 1, 3, and 6 are mentioned in the rubrics as especially appropriate for this celebration. Continuing the eschatological note sounded in the first exhortation of the service, the opening words of the institution narrative are changed to emphasize that *this* is the night. With Prayer 3 the presider has the option of using one of the prefaces for Holy Week. Prayer 1 connects the blood of Jesus' new covenant with the wider sweep of salvation history. Prayer 6 extends that historical overview into even fuller expression. The theme of love is again evoked in various ways: "your mighty works reveal your wisdom and love"; "that we might live no longer for ourselves, but for him who died and rose for us"; "having loved his own who were in the world, he loved them to the end."

Though the Prayer after Communion concludes the liturgy proper, a number of other things often follow.

If the sacrament is to be reserved for communion the next day, a procession forms to carry it to the altar of repose, a place where the faithful may gather to pray and worship Christ substantially present. The vessels containing the sacrament should be simple: a flagon of wine, a plate with bread on it, or a ciborium of wafers. The procession may consist of thurifer, crucifer, servers carrying tapers, and minister(s) carrying the sacrament. A eucharistic hymn may be sung during the procession.

After the sacrament has been placed at the altar of repose, the ministers may leave, without further ceremony, to remove their vestments. Ornaments in the church and cloths on the altar may now be removed. As this happens, Psalm 22, and the account of Jesus' agony in the garden (Mathew 26:30–46), may be read. There are no further prayers, blessings, or dismissals. The church may be darkened, the only lights being those that are kept at the altar of repose. The congregation leaves in silence.

In some places, it is the custom to maintain a prayer vigil before the sacrament, either through the entire night, with people taking shifts, or until midnight. Such a vigil provides an opportunity for people to express their love of Christ and gratitude for the gift of himself in the eucharist. If, however, it becomes a matter of weighing the relative merits of an extended vigil on Maundy Thursday and a long vigil on Easter Eve, it would be preferable by far to put the energy into the Great Vigil. That period of watching, waiting, song, and praise deserves the greater weight.

It is important to note that some portion of the sacrament should be reserved in a place apart in the building in case of emergency. This may be in a sacristy or vestry. It is not necessary to provide lights or veils.

Good Friday

When I am lifted up from the earth, I will draw all things to myself," Jesus prophesied before his Passion (John 12:32). "I will champion every one's cause, I will bear the whole burden of human guilt, I will restore fallen human nature to its original integrity. In me all sickness will be cured and all wounds healed.

St. Leo the Great, Sermon LVI on the Passion

In the first centuries of the church, the Christian Passover was not divided into separate "packages"; rather, it was seen as a unitive commemoration of the death and resurrection of Jesus, celebrating both his passage from death to life and the Christian's own share in that victory through baptism.

Seen in this context, as part of the larger celebration of the Paschal Mystery, it is appropriate that the ceremonial of Good Friday provide an opportunity for austere meditation on the Passion and cross of Jesus, as well as solemn prayer for the church and the world for which he died. But the liturgy should not give the appearance of being "Jesus' funeral," complete with gloomy hymns. Moreover, the austerity of the ceremonial should not preclude a note (or even a chord) of triumph and joy, for the community gathers on Good Friday to *celebrate* the Lord's triumph on the cross — an event that can only be understood from the viewpoint of Easter.

Colour: Passion Red

Items Needed for the Service

- the altar and chancel area remain bare, everything having been removed at the end of the Maundy Thursday liturgy
- (if there is to be the Meditation on the Cross) a large wooden cross in a convenient location from which it may be brought into the church with ease and dignity
- two lighted candles (on long candlesticks or stands) to be placed on either side of the cross after it is brought into the church
- (if the reserved sacrament is to be administered) one or more chalices and (possibly) extra patens or baskets for distributing the reserved eucharistic bread;
- purificators and a folded corporal placed on the credence table
- alb or cassock and surplice (the use of black cassocks alone is to be discouraged, since the cassock is not a liturgical vestment); if other vestments are worn, the colour should be that of Holy Week; black tippets are not used

The Gathering of the Community

There is no opening hymn. The people stand as the minister(s) enter(s) in silence and bows before the altar. In some places the ancient tradition of prostration before the altar is continued as a sign of deep humility in the face of the mystery being celebrated. Such a prostration should be practised carefully in advance so that it is carried out gracefully and in unison if there is more than one minister. The ministers proceed to their places (or remain before the altar), and the opening versicles and responses are said, followed by a profound silence, and the penitential prayer. The presider greets the community with "The Lord be with you" and sings or says the collect. All sit for the readings.

The Proclamation of the Word

The readings do not vary from year to year. The psalm could be sung to a simple chant without accompaniment. Indeed, it would be appropriate, and quite effective, to reduce instrumental accompaniment to a minimum, or even omit it altogether. The Passion Gospel (John 18:1–19:42) or the shorter version (John 19:17–30) is begun and concluded without the usual acclamations. Because the evangelist clearly thought that the whole story was worth telling, the longer version is really to be preferred. If this is thought to be a long time for the congregation to stand, people may remain seated until Jesus' arrival at Golgotha (John 19:17). A notice explaining this could be placed in the leaflet, and the narrator could give a simple gesture indicating that the congregation should rise. (Servers, choir, and other ministers can assist by being prepared in advance to give the lead in standing at this point.)

The narrative can be read or sung in parts. While it has been the custom in many places for the congregation to assume the part of the crowd, this is a questionable practice. The evangelist's intention was not to induce guilt ("We did this"), but to encourage faith. With this in mind, a smaller group could take the part of the crowd to allow the congregation to hear the whole story. At the words telling of Jesus' death (19:30), the narrator should pause to allow silent meditation. After the reading of the Passion, another silence may be kept. This is followed by a homily based on the readings. The preacher should try to express both the joy and the solemnity of the occasion. A hymn may follow the homily.

The Solemn Intercessions

The Solemn Intercessions (or prayers for the whole family of God) have been a part of the Good Friday liturgy since early times. The order of the petitions can be found as far back as the liturgy of the fifth-century Roman church. In these prayers, the church holds up before God all for whom Christ died.

The deacon or other person appointed to lead the prayers calls the community to pray for specific concerns through a series of biddings. The congregation may stand for the biddings and kneel for the silence and collects, or simply remain standing or kneeling. The deacon directs the action ("Let us stand," "Let us kneel"). A generous silence should follow the bidding. The presider then prays the collect. The presider may remain at the chair with the deacon alongside, or the ministers may face the people from some other position (possibly the chancel steps). In some places, it is the custom for the deacon to stand in the midst of the congregation while the presider remains at the chair. The service may be concluded after the Solemn Intercessions with the Lord's Prayer, a hymn, and the final prayer (p. 320).

The five sets of biddings and collects, while not containing any specific references to the cross and Passion, make clear the meaning of the crucifixion. The final collect, moreover, prays that the "whole world" may look to the church as a sign of God's love. Thus, in the cross, all humanity is brought together.

Meditation on the Cross of Jesus

The rubrics suggest that a wooden cross be carried in for this portion of the liturgy. This custom is first attested to by the pilgrim nun, Egeria. She relates that on Good Friday in Jerusalem the people gathered to venerate a relic of the cross. The bishop held the wood at both ends, and deacons stood on guard about him lest there be a repetition of the case of a devout soul who bit off a piece of the cross and made off with it. The people filed past, touching the wood of the cross with their foreheads, kissing it, and moving on.

If desired, torches, or candles may be placed on either side of the cross. The cross may be placed upright in a stand, or placed against the chancel step or rail. The cross should, ideally, be large and rough-hewn — a small brass cross or crucifix is not appropriate! The presider may carry the cross (possibly accompanied by the torch bearers) from the narthex or sacristy (vestry). The verse and response (p. 313) are said or sung at the beginning of the procession, halfway to the chancel, and at the chancel. The presider may slightly elevate the cross at each station, as she or he proclaims the versicle. Or the cross may be carried in silence, with the versicle proclaimed just before the cross is set in its resting place.

The *BAS* sacramentary provides three chant settings of the verse and response. Careful preparation by presider and choir are necessary if this beautiful music is to be well done. Because it is heard by a congregation only once a year, or it is new to them, advance work must be done if the people are going to be able to respond, "Come, let us worship."

During the adoration of the crucified one, anthems and hymns may be sung (see pp. 314–317 for examples), although there should also be periods of silence for meditation. Some members of the congregation may wish to come forward to bow or kneel before the cross, to touch it or to kiss it as a sign of devotion to Christ. If this custom is new to the community, the presider should explain its significance and be the first to venerate the cross, followed by others who have been prepared to give a lead to the congregation. It may be pointed out that the cross is a throne, and the veneration of the cross is not unlike the homage given to a sovereign. After a decent period of time, the Meditation on the Cross ends with a hymn. "Sing, my tongue, the glorious battle" (*Pange lingua gloriosa certaminis*) is specifically recommended, as it makes clear that the scene on Golgotha was a battle that ended in victory. The service may end here with the Lord's Prayer and the final prayer (p. 320).

The Holy Communion

In places where it is the custom to celebrate the eucharist, the ceremonial continues with the preparation of the gifts, and the eucharist is celebrated according to local custom. The *BAS* does not discuss the relative merits or drawbacks of a eucharistic celebration on Good Friday. In its favour, one might turn in the first place to Paul's statement that the eucharist is a proclamation of the Lord's death until he comes (1 Cor: 11–26). Good Friday might thus seem a pre-eminent occasion for the eucharist.

The more widespread practice of the western church, however, has been to administer communion from sacrament reserved at the Maundy Thursday eucharist. This practice, unique in the year, has the advantage of highlighting Good Friday's special character. What is offered on the cross for the life of the world is received in broken bread and shared wine that still bear the prints of the prayer for unity and service Christ uttered the night before. It is that bread that must sustain us through the *kenosis*[30] of the entombment of Christ and his descent among the dead. The eucharist is not celebrated at all on Holy Saturday. This extended celebration of the Paschal Mystery leads to the offering of the sacrifice of praise and thanksgiving once again at the Great Vigil. This makes particular sense especially if that eucharist takes place early on Easter Sunday morning. Of course, in practice, in those places where the Vigil has been revived, the eucharist probably will take place before midnight. (For further discussion regarding the timing of the Vigil, see the section on The Great Vigil of Easter.)

If the practice of administering holy communion reserved from the Maundy Thursday eucharist is used, this order may be followed:

The cross (and torches) may need to be moved, but should not be *re-moved* (i.e., the cross should still dominate the liturgical space in some way). A corporal or fair linen may be spread on the altar, and the vessels arranged on it by the deacon or assisting minister. The reserved sacrament should be brought to the altar in silence by the presider or another minister. The presider introduces and begins the Lord's Prayer (p. 318). If there is to be more than one minister assisting at communion, the presider pours the consecrated wine (from a flagon or other vessel used for reservation) into chalices and divides the bread into containers. Holy Communion is administered in silence according to local custom.

After communion, the vessels are removed to the credence table or sacristy. The ablutions are done after the conclusion of

---

30 The "emptying." See Philipians 2:7.

the liturgy. The final prayers are said (one of the prayers on page 319, followed by the prayer on page 320).

There is no blessing or dismissal. The ministers leave in silence. The cross (and candles) remain in place. The community may be encouraged (obviously at a time before the end of the service) to remain (or return) for silent meditation on the cross. They should also be reminded (again at an earlier point in the liturgy) that Good Friday does not stand on its own, but is part of one event: the death and resurrection of Jesus Christ.

HOLY SATURDAY

Something strange is happening — there is a great silence on earth today, a great silence and stillness. The whole earth keeps silence because the king is asleep. The earth trembled and is still because God has fallen asleep in the flesh and he has raised up all who have slept since the world began. God has died in the flesh and hell trembles with fear.

From an ancient homily on the holy and great Sabbath, PG 43

COLOUR: PASSION RED

The tone of Holy Saturday is one of waiting, watching, expectation, and rest. It is the Sabbath Day *par excellence* of the Christian year. Holy Saturday commemorates the repose of Christ in the tomb and his descent among the dead. The eucharist is not celebrated on this day.

Historically, in most parts of the church, there has been no special liturgy for this day, though the daily offices are prayed as usual. In some parts of the church, however (specifically Milan and parts of Gaul in the post-Nicene era), a special Liturgy of the Word developed. In recent centuries, it has been a uniquely Anglican tradition to have a Liturgy of the Word without the eucharist — something preserved in both the *BAS* and *The Book of Common Prayer* of the Episcopal church.[31] The *BAS* provides a

[31] Marion Hatchett's *Commentary on the American Prayer Book* (New York: Seabury Press, 1980), 238-239, provides a brief discussion of this liturgy.

collect and a set of lections with no explicit instructions regarding their use. These propers, however, match those in the Episcopal Prayer Book, which provides more detail for a Liturgy of the Word. This liturgy begins with the Collect of the Day. The Prayers of the People are replaced by the Anthem, "In the midst of life we are in death," and concludes with the Lord's Prayer and the Grace.

The tone of the liturgy should match that of the day: quiet and unadorned. Any music that might be used, for the psalm or anthem, should be simple and, if at all possible, unaccompanied. Church decoration remains as it was for the Good Friday liturgy, with everything stripped bare. While candles may have been placed on the altar for communion on Good Friday, they are not used during this liturgy. The vestments of the presider are kept as simple as possible. Cassock, surplus, and stole are a good option. The presider and any other assisting ministers occupy the places they normally would for the Liturgy of the Word at the eucharist.

It must be admitted that the Liturgy of the Word on Holy Saturday has not been widely used by any but a very few parishes, seminaries, or religious communities. The already extensive schedule for Holy Week tends to work against anything else being done on this day. In most churches, there is a fair amount of activity going on to prepare for the Great Vigil and Easter Sunday, with rehearsals for servers, sidespeople, readers, and others, along with the preparations of the altar guild. Where this liturgy is celebrated, however, the experience has provided a quiet reflective "tone setter" for the other preparations of the day. The simplicity, starkness, and brevity of the liturgy make it easy to put together. Parishes interested in using this liturgy might consider inviting those involved in rehearsals or other preparations to come half an hour earlier than normal to begin their day with prayer. A simple description of the liturgy with a short background commentary, relating the day to the commemoration of the repose of Christ in the tomb, would help parishioners understand the significance of the event.

Items Needed for the Service

- alb or cassock and surplice
- Bible or lectionary
- service books

The Gathering of the Community

The presider and any assisting ministers enter in silence, and the people are asked by the deacon or other minister to kneel in silent prayer. After a period of silence, the people are asked to stand and the Collect of the Day is prayed.

The Proclamation of the Word

The Liturgy of the Word then proceeds as usual. Since there is no "Alleluia" or other music between the Epistle reading and the Gospel, silence may be kept or a tract may be sung (Psalm 130 is particularly appropriate). The usual responses before and after the Gospel are also dropped, and the Gospel is introduced with the words, "The conclusion of the Passion of our Lord Jesus Christ according to ..." The Gospel may be followed by a homily, a reading from one of the ancient homilies on Holy Saturday (an example is provided at the end of this section), or a period of silent reflection. The creed is not recited.

Reflecting the focus on the repose of Christ in the tomb, elements from the burial service have often been a part of Holy Saturday. A possible substitute for Prayers of the People might be as follows.

> The anthem "In the midst of life" (p. 576) may be said or sung. The refrain "Holy God ..." can be replaced with the form from the Episcopal *BCP*, 1979:

Holy God, Holy and Mighty,
Holy and merciful Saviour,
deliver us not into the bitterness of eternal death.

or

Lord Jesus Christ, by your death you took away the sting of death (p. 602).

or

As a concluding collect, or in place of an element from the burial service, the second post-communion prayer for Good Friday may be said: "Lord Jesus Christ, Son of the Living God ..." (p. 319).

The liturgy is concluded with the Lord's Prayer and the dismissal ("Let us bless the Lord," "Thanks be to God") or the Grace. The presider and assisting ministers leave in silence.

THE GREAT VIGIL OF EASTER

Rejoice, heavenly powers! Sing, choirs of angels! Exult, all creation around God's throne! Jesus Christ, our King, is risen! Sound the trumpet of salvation ...
This is our Passover feast, when Christ, the true Lamb, is slain, whose blood consecrates the homes of all believers.
This is the night when first you saved our forebears: you freed the people of Israel from their slavery and led them dry-shod through the sea.
This is the night when Christians everywhere, washed clean of sin and freed from all defilement, are restored to grace and grow together in holiness.
This is the night when Jesus Christ broke the chains of death and rose triumphant from the grave ...
Night truly blessed when heaven is wedded to earth and we are reconciled with God!"

Excerpts from the Exsultet, *BAS,* p. 323

The earliest and most central celebration of the resurrection in the Christian church was, and is, the observance of the first day of the week, "The Lord's Day," the day on which Christ rose from the dead. There is no evidence to suggest that Christians in the New Testament era, or even in the generations following, observed an annual Sunday as The Day of the Resurrection. What we know as Easter actually began with the celebration of the Jewish Passover by those who became Christians. Whether Christians of the New Testament era observed a special or distinct Passover is not clear. St. Paul's reference to "Christ our Passover" may be an indication of such a celebration, or it may be the beginnings of theologizing by Jewish Christians who more and more began to see the death and resurrection of Jesus as the culmination of God's work of salvation, which was celebrated at Passover. Whatever the case, it is clear that in the second century Christians began observing a "Christian Passover," coinciding with the Jewish Passover but completely transformed by Christian belief and the centrality of Christ's death and resurrection.

Like the Jewish Passover, the Christian liturgy was observed at night. Beginning after sundown, it involved readings from Scripture and preaching on the significance of Christ's suffering, death, and resurrection. It focused on the theology of Christ as the Passover lamb, and ended sometime in the early hours of the morning with a celebration of the eucharist. The celebration was soon moved to the Saturday night following Passover, in order to coincide with the Lord's Day and thus add further significance to the event. Baptisms began to be collected to this celebration, and it became the single most significant event in the Christian year. St. Augustine refers to it as the "Mother of all Vigils." Tertullian (*c.* 160 to *c.* 225), in discussing the advisability of Christian women marrying pagan men, demonstrates the importance placed on the Great Vigil. He recommends against such marriages on the grounds that pagan husbands might not permit their wives to attend this all-night event.

Various elements of the Vigil were added through the following centuries. With the virtual disappearance of adult baptismal candidates, a significant dimension of the Vigil was lost. In addition, the length and timing of the celebration led to dwindling attendance. The Vigil was greatly shortened and the emphasis shifted to the morning of Easter Day. By the high Middle Ages, the Vigil had become little more than a vestige.

The recovery of the Vigil as the heart of the Easter celebration and the Christian year goes hand in hand with the recovery of the Paschal Mystery at the heart of Christian faith. It is an event in which movement, colour, darkness and light, fire and water, songs and stories, food and drink are all brought together to allow us, once again, to celebrate the Christian Passover — the story of how God has brought us out of slavery and darkness into freedom and light in Jesus Christ.

An inescapable dimension of the Vigil is its nocturnal character. While many congregations cheerfully look forward to the Christmas "midnight" service (even if it sometimes begins as early as 9:00 p.m.), encouraging people to come to a lengthy liturgy on Holy Saturday night remains a challenge. If the celebration begins before sundown or before it is truly dark, the impact of a most effective feature of the service — the lighting of the new fire and the Paschal Candle — is lost. Similarly, if the primary concern becomes brevity, the sense of duration, of watching and waiting, is lost. The Vigil is a service in which participants will be fairly marinated in Scripture. This takes time.

Given the limitations of frail flesh, one possibility is to invite people to attend three liturgies: a service of light with the new fire (in the evening), a service of four or five lections with their attendant psalmody and prayer (also in the evening), and the first eucharist of Easter (on the following morning). After the first service, those who need to return home would leave, and a smaller group could remain. This group might convene each hour through the night to listen to readings, sing, and pray. The larger group could then return a little before sunrise for the baptisms and/or the renewal of vows and the eucharist. If the timing is right, the growing light will speak compellingly of the risen Christ.

Colour: White

Preparation

Because of the variety and amount of activity involved in the Vigil, and because it is celebrated only once a year, thorough preparation and planning are crucial to make it the solemn act of worship it is intended to be. A number of things can be done to ensure that details and logistics do not obscure the central elements of the liturgy.

Orders of Service

Since the Vigil is lengthy and is not the regular liturgy of the community, an expanded service leaflet is recommended to help guide the congregation. Printing all the congregational parts, including music for the psalms, hymns, baptismal covenant, and service music (*Sanctus*, *Agnus Dei*, etc.), removes the need for handling many books and will ultimately make the congregation feel more at ease with what is going on. From the presider's perspective, it also obviates the need to announce page numbers for people to follow along. Readings, collects, and other parts that the presider reads or prays alone are best left out; first, because the congregation is thereby enabled to listen collectively to what is being said, rather than getting buried in reading a text; second, because the leaflet then remains a manageable size. The presider's parts might also be collected into a single binder for ease of use during the liturgy. (In practice, using the sacramentary requires some skilful juggling of page turns.) If this is done, the binder should appear attractive and appropriate to the occasion.

The Great Vigil will provide people with vivid memories of a "special night." Because Sunday is the primary weekly celebration of the Paschal Mystery, any allusions or associations that can be made in appearance, order, or ceremonial to connect the Vigil with Sunday worship, will serve as a continuing reminder to the congregation throughout the year. Keeping church furnishings such as Paschal Candle stands, presider's chair, altar, and font in their usual locations, and placing liturgical elements such as baptisms in the same position where they occur in the Sunday eucharist, will help to make these connections.

Congregational involvement in the planning and implementation of any liturgy is usually desirable. The Easter Vigil is no exception. In places where the Vigil is new, involving more people in the planning stages will promote an openness to the service and an understanding of what it is and why it is done. Some groups, such as choir, servers, altar guild, readers, and intercessors, will automatically be involved. Members of the parish worship committee can also appropriately take part in selecting the hymns and the readings from the Old Testament, and in considering how various parts of the Vigil can be done most effectively, given the architectural space.

Training and rehearsals are vital. Normally competent servers can be overwhelmed by the number of tasks to be remembered and performed, and dim light during the Service of Light and the Vigil can add to the confusion of where to be when. People who normally read quite well with little practice may find the low light a problem and need significantly more rehearsal, both for reading and for moving from place to place. Walking through the liturgy ahead of time, from beginning to end, is highly recommended. Because of the number of people involved, it is usually better to hold separate rehearsals for servers, readers, baptismal candidates (and families), sidespeople, and any other groups who are to play a part in the liturgy. Rehearsing the groups separately allows people to focus on their own part and not become distracted or daunted by all the details that will occupy others.

If the rehearsals are to be effective, the presider must have carefully worked through every detail in advance. A Master of Ceremonies is also recommended (though not necessary). Having someone else take on some of the responsibility for rehearsing the participants — and for directing the liturgy in progress — allows the presider, deacon, and others to concentrate on their own parts rather than worrying whether everyone else is in the right place at the right time.

Items Needed for the Service

- Paschal Candle (possibly with nails or incense, and dates)
- fuel and a vessel for the new fire
- altar vested in white
- white chasuble or white stole
- sacramentary
- Bible or lectionary book
- hand candles for congregation
- small flashlight

- matches
- lighter or flint and steel
- water for font
- towels
- baptismal candles(s)
- chrism
- [*aspergillum* or branch for sprinkling of congregation]
- [thurible and incense]

The various elements of the liturgy involve the use of a significant number of items which need to be properly arranged in advance. Some of these, such as materials for baptism and the eucharist, may be determined by the normal parish practice, but others require more detailed comment. (It may also be noted that the Vigil, because of its solemnity, may be a good time to enhance the usual ritual actions by introducing immersions for baptism, the use of chrism at the sign of the cross, etc.)

The Great Vigil begins with the lighting of the new fire. While it may seem to be an easy task to light a fire, it can be a hazardous exercise and potentially disastrous. There are many stories of overly ambitious fires that have had to die down before they could be approached for the lighting of the Paschal Candle or, conversely, fires that were so cautiously built that they left little impression on the congregation, or even went out before candles could be lit from them. For these reasons it is a very good idea to rehearse setting the fire. Thought should be given to the type of vessel in which the fire will be lit, whether a Hibachi, a barbecue, a wok, or some other heavy pot or container, such as a steel wastepaper basket. If a Hibachi or other smaller container is used, it should be placed on a table to provide easier access and greater visibility during the liturgy. Weather and the location, either inside or outside, are considerations in planning for the size of the fire (and thus the container). Outdoor fires have the benefit of being larger, but should not be so large as to become unmanageable for lighting candles (or charcoal for incense). Indoor fires need to be smaller for safety and ventilation, but they also need to last long enough to light the candles, and to be substantial enough for the congregation to see.

In order that the fire be genuinely "new," some people light it with flint and steel; others use simply a lighter or matches. Whatever method is chosen, the person who is to light the fire should be able to do so without going through dozens of matches or taking a long time to get a few sparks from flint and steel to ignite. It is recommended that the fire be set up in its place and lit in a test run, so that any difficulties can be dealt with before the liturgy begins. It may be necessary to make arrangements for the fire to be smothered after the liturgy has moved on, especially if its location and size pose a threat to safety when unattended. Likewise, if the fire is to be lit indoors, plan to turn off any smoke detectors before the liturgy begins and to turn them on after. Smoke alarms can be disruptive!

The Paschal Candle is lit from the new fire. After the procession into the church, the candle is placed in its stand for the readings. The deacon or another minister removes the candles and carries it to the font for baptism. A good time to form a procession to the font may be during the litany for the baptismal candidates. The deacon leads the procession, holding a candle. An ancient custom has the presider dipping the candle three times into the font during the Thanksgiving over the Water (in the *BAS* at the words "Now sanctify this water ..."). Following the baptism(s), the deacon replaces the candle in its stand. It is important that the Paschal Candle be fitted properly in its stand ahead of time, and that the wax be trimmed or the base adjusted so that placement and removal can be accomplished without a struggle.

The *BAS* describes how the Paschal Candle may be carved and ornamented to stress its significance. A cross, the Greek letters *Alpha* and *Omega*, and the date may be inscribed, and nails or grains of incense inserted (p. 333). If this is done, the markings should be traced and the small holes for nails or incense should be made in advance, to facilitate the process during the liturgy. A rounded wax surface can be difficult to carve, and an even more difficult medium in which to embed incense grains, especially if the presider is attempting to read the appropriate words at the same time. If the candle is to have a follower, it is best to light the candle in advance and set the follower properly in place. Some Paschal Candles come with wax numbers, which are probably best glued on before the liturgy and traced over during the ceremony. Dates provided in the form of decals should also be applied in advance.

The placement of the Paschal Candle stand is important, as the candle is one of the major symbols in the Vigil, representing the light of the risen Christ. The stand should be placed at the front of the church in a prominent place, either in the middle of the sanctuary or near the lectern. Those planning the service could test a number of locations for visibility and prominence, keeping in mind that the candle should not obscure the congregation's view of liturgical action at the altar during the eucharist. Since the candle is meant to be lit at services throughout the Easter season, it might best be placed where it will not have to be moved for regular Sunday liturgies.

Ten readings from the Old Testament are provided, and at least three are to be read. The selection from Exodus is always to be included. The readings should be chosen with an understanding that the Vigil is not simply an expanded Liturgy of the Word for a eucharist. The readings are baptismal "types," foreshadowing our own baptism through which we enter the path of salvation. While three readings are the specified minimum, five would be more likely to accomplish the task of proclaiming the magnitude of God's saving work. The greater the number of readings, the longer the liturgy. But a few words at the beginning of the service to explain the significance of the Vigil can be very helpful in setting people at ease and freeing them from our painfully time-conscious culture.

There are, then, a number of readings to be marked at the lectern. Since these readings are usually read by candlelight, they will need to be well marked and, if possible, specially prepared. They might be provided on tabbed looseleaf sheets and collected in an attractive binder. If the level of light is particularly low, a small flashlight could be useful; or if the location and configuration of the lectern warrant, a pair of candles might be placed on either side.

If incense and *asperges* are to be used during the service, the materials should be set out in advance. Generally the charcoal for the incense to be used in the procession with the Paschal Candle is lit from the new fire. The coals can be placed among the material to be burned. When they catch, they are immediately removed with tongs and placed in the thurible. Alternatively, a couple of coals can be lit and put in the thurible in advance.

The *asperges* (sprinkling of the congregation with water from the font) takes place after the baptism(s) to remind all present of their own baptisms. A vessel for the *asperges* can be filled with water from the font. The presider may use a pine bough to sprinkle the people, as it will hold a good amount of water and can be wielded to great effect. Some parishes follow the practice of censing or sprinkling the new fire as part of the blessing (as with the palms on the Sunday of the Passion). Sprinkling the fire may be inadvisable because of the conflicting symbolism. In any event, too much water will put the fire out!

The Gathering of the Community

Just before the liturgy is to begin, the presider (or someone else, such as a Master of Ceremonies) might give a short introduction. It does not have to be detailed, but might simply outline for the congregation the overall movement and tone of the liturgy, placing the length of the service, for example, in context. People can even be invited to remove their watches and allow themselves to live in the liturgy, to experience a sense of duration and waiting, rather than worrying about time. They may need some direction regarding the procession with the Paschal Candle. (On the other hand, this is not an occasion to rehearse music or other parts of the liturgy. If there is a significant amount of music to be learned, it would be best to rehearse it sometime in Lent.)

The Order of the Vigil

The Great Vigil consists of four parts: the Service of Light, the Liturgy of the Word, Christian Initiation or the Renewal of Baptismal Vows, and The Holy Eucharist with the administration of Easter Communion. At various times in the church's history these elements have been arranged in a number of different ways. The *BAS* specifies the order as the Service of Light, the Liturgy of the Word, and the first Easter eucharist with the Glory to God and with baptisms or reaffirmation of baptismal vows occurring where they would in a normal baptismal liturgy. Although the *BAS* does not provide a rationale for this particular order, a number of points can be made that support it.

The Service of Light, which includes the lighting of the Paschal Candle, the procession, and the singing of the *Exsultet*, is derived from the practical necessity of lighting lamps in the growing darkness at dusk. The early church quickly came to associate this action with the image of Christ as the light of the world, and began the practice of singing a hymn to the light. The lamp-lighting became a part of evening prayer. Because the Great Vigil began at sundown, the lighting of lamps naturally formed the starting point for the all-night Vigil. Over time, the special status of the Vigil lent a greater solemnity to the lamp-lighting on this night, and the Paschal Candle and *Exsultet* became fixtures of the rite.

Reversing the order by placing the Liturgy of the Word before the Service of Light (an option on page 334) suggests that the readings from the Old Testament are entirely preparatory to the presence of Christ. The readings are seen as an account of salvation history leading to the Paschal Mystery. But the significance and elaboration of the Service of Light at the Vigil lend weight to preserving its place of origin at the beginning, as a lighting of candles in preparation for the Vigil, and especially as a reminder that the whole Vigil occurs in the presence of the risen Lord. Likewise, while the words of the *Exsultet* do in fact speak of the resurrection, the climax of the resurrection proclamation comes later, with the Easter acclamation and Glory to God, or as some suggest, with the Alleluia and Gospel.[32]

The baptismal portion of the liturgy has also occurred in various places throughout the service. The order as given in the *BAS* helps connect the pattern for baptism at the Vigil with baptisms at other times of the year. This order, by placing the baptisms after the liturgical proclamations of the resurrection, reflects the historical reality that all Christians are baptized as a response to the experience of the resurrected Christ.

The Service of Light

The Great Vigil of Easter (as outlined in the *BAS)* normally begins with the Service of Light. This may take place at an appropriate place outside the church building (weather permitting), in the church hall or basement, or at the back of the church itself. Architecture and ventilation for the fire will play a part, but the ability to process easily with a lit Paschal Candle is also an important factor. The procession with the lit candle entering a darkened church represents Christ as the light, leading his people to life in the midst of a darkened world. It also represents his antetype, the pillar of light leading the Israelites through the wilderness to their liberation.

---

32 Rupert Berger and Hans Hollerweger, eds., translated by Matthew J. O'Connell, *Celebrating the Easter Vigil* (New York: Pueblo, 1983), 112. The Rev. Dr. John Gibaut has argued that the Vigil "shows its seams," the result of different components being conjoined over many centuries. If the Vigil is to be, in fact, a "Great Sunday," he argues that the *Exsultet* effectively takes the place of the Gloria. He would argue then that the next phase of revision of the Vigil would see the elimination of the Gloria altogether. The service would move from Vigil readings to the Romans 6 reading, followed by the Great Alleluia, Gospel, baptisms, and so on.

If at all possible, the lighting of the fire takes place in complete darkness. A small penlight or flashlight usually gives sufficient light for striking the match, flint, or lighter. Once the fire has caught, the presider proceeds with the address beginning, "Dear friends in Christ ..." followed by the prayer over the fire. (During this time, the thurifer should remove lighted charcoal from the fire and place it in the thurible.) A small taper should be lit from the fire and kept burning until the Paschal Candle is readied.

Once the prayer is completed, the Paschal Candle is brought to the presider, who cuts (or traces) the cross and letters in the candle, and inserts the nails or incense while reciting the accompanying words (p. 333). The candle is then lit using the small taper, accompanied by the words provided ("May the light ...").

The procession with the Paschal Candle now begins with the first acclamation. The deacon (or priest, if there is no deacon) faces those gathered, lifts the candle high, and sings, "The light of Christ." (See the *BAS* sacramentary, pp. 267–268.) After the congregation has responded, the deacon leads the way into the church with thurifer, crucifer, torches, bookbearers, and any other assistants following. At a second station midway to the candlestand, the deacon again turns to the congregation, lifts the candle high, and sings the acclamation, with the congregation responding. The procession then moves to the Paschal Candle stand, where the acclamation and response are repeated for the last time. The candle is placed in its stand and other lights may be lit (such as hand candles for the congregation). Some people light hand candles from the Paschal Candle as soon as it has been lit. While this is an option (in some places necessary to avoid tripping in the dark), leaving the Paschal Candle as the only light during the procession intensifies the symbolic act of following the single light of Christ in the darkness, thus heightening the impact. (Another possible variation is to begin lighting the congregation's candles at the second station, or, if the congregation is to remain in its place, candles can be lit in different sections of the congregation as the procession makes its way forward.)

If incense is being used, the thurifer brings the thurible to the deacon to cense the Paschal Candle immediately before the *Exsultet*.

The deacon, or an appointed cantor, stands next to the candle and sings the *Exsultet* while the congregation remains standing. Extra light can be provided by processional torches held by servers at either side of the book. Music for the *Exsultet* can be found in the *BAS* sacramentary (pp. 268ff). The *Exsultet* is a beautiful but challenging piece of music for which ample rehearsal is absolutely necessary. While it is the deacon's prerogative to sing the *Exsultet*, practical necessity may require that the best available singer take on the task. If there is no one who can sing the piece, a congregational hymn such as "Jesus Christ is risen today" may be substituted. A parish might also experiment with a modern setting of the *Exsultet*, in place of the traditional plainsong. When the *Exsultet* has been sung, the congregation's hand candles may be extinguished, or they may be kept burning as a source of light during the Liturgy of the Word. Light from candles makes more of an impact than artificial light.

The Proclamation of the Word

The lectern from which the lections are read should be in a prominent and visible place, as should the presider who is to pray the collects and preside visibly over the liturgy. The best option is usually for the presider to sit where she or he would normally sit for the Liturgy of the Word at the eucharist.

The Liturgy of the Word begins after the singing of the *Exsultet*, when the whole congregation has sat down. The people remain seated during the readings and psalms, standing only to pray the collects. After each reading, a silence is kept. The silence is broken by the choir or other musicians who are leading the singing of the psalm. At the end of the psalm, the presider immediately reads the appointed collect. Two torchbearers may stand on either side of the presider to provide light. To keep activity to a minimum during the silences, readers can remain standing at the lectern until the prayer is completed.

A moment of silence is kept after the last collect is prayed. This is followed by the singing of a hymn of praise, such as the Gloria or "You are God." In some places, the silence is broken by singing the Easter Acclamation "Alleluia, Christ is Risen … The Lord is risen indeed, Alleluia!" followed by the ringing of bells, improvisation on the organ, or whatever other celebratory sounds seem appropriate. Members of the congregation can be asked in advance to bring their own bells to join in the celebration. The hymn of praise begins after a few minutes of such "holy noise."[33]

Baptism and the Renewal of Baptismal Vows

Once the singing of the hymn is completed, the service continues with the Collect of the Day, the Epistle, and the Gospel reading. In keeping with the solemnity of the Great Vigil, it is particularly appropriate to have a full Gospel procession. The sermon follows the Gospel reading. Different parishes have different customs and expectations regarding the length, style, and content of sermons. The extensive amount of Scripture read at the Easter Vigil, along with the *Exsultet* and the theological reflection offered by the renewal of baptismal vows, suggest a brief and concise homily.

Holy Baptism begins after the sermon, and can proceed in much the same way it does during the rest of the year, with a few added considerations. Having a baptism within the context of the Easter Vigil is a good opportunity for parishes to rethink their liturgical practice around this sacrament.

Normally the Paschal Candle is placed at the front of the church, which may or may not be near the font. If the font is not near the Paschal Candle, then the deacon or a server may carry the Paschal Candle in procession to the font, leading the baptismal party. This may also be done at subsequent baptisms during the rest of the year, in imitation of the Vigil. On these occasions, the

---

[33] If the community follows the order suggested in the previous footnote, the "holy noise" takes place during the Alleluia before the Gospel.

Paschal Candle is placed in its Easter location at the front, before the service begins.

The Vigil setting suggests the extravagant use of symbol to convey the meaning and power of the sacramental rite. Parishes may therefore consider baptism by full immersion. If this is not practical, a catchment basin or pool large enough to stand in may be constructed of waterproof sheets and blocks of wood, or even a children's wading pool (if appropriately disguised), and placed on the floor by the font. Large quantities of water can be poured into such a receptacle. Experience has shown that this practice can greatly enhance the congregation's appreciation for and understanding of the importance of this primary sacrament. Once begun at the Vigil, such a practice can often be continued as a normal part of the baptismal liturgy. If more than just a few drops of water are used to baptize candidates, they will need time to dry off and change their clothing. The newly baptized can be vested in albs, symbolic of having "put on Christ." Infants can be clothed in their christening gowns (now, rather than before the baptism). This best takes place before the giving of the light. While the congregation is waiting for the candidates' return, anthems, chants, or hymns may be sung.

The congregation may be sprinkled with water from the font after the candidates have been baptized, and while they are changing their clothes. In this particular context, the *asperges* are best understood as a sensory reminder to the whole congregation that they are a community of the baptized that has just renewed its own baptismal covenant. As noted above, a jug or bowl to scoop water from the font will be needed, so that the whole congregation can be sprinkled, unless people are able to gather around the font for the baptisms. A pine bough or an *aspergillum* works well for the sprinkling. Again, if this is indeed to work as a "sensory reminder" of baptism, significant amounts of water should be used.

The *BAS* provides the option of using *chrism* when making the sign of the cross on the forehead of baptismal candidates (p. 160). The use of *chrism* at baptism is an ancient tradition of the church, symbolizing the gift of the anointing of the Spirit. There are many allusions to the use of oil in the Bible, including the anointing of kings and priests. Perhaps its significance is best explained by the words of the eucharistic prayer used at the service during which the *chrism* is blessed by the bishop:

> Blessed are you, gracious God, creator of heaven and earth; for you anointed your Son Jesus Christ with the Holy Spirit and with power; and you anoint us with the same Spirit in baptism, making us a holy people in the royal priesthood of the new covenant. (p. 619)

Chrism is normally made of olive oil scented with balsam. Other aromatic oils may also be used, but it is important that the scent be pleasant. Anointing with scented oil is intended to demonstrate the richness of God's extravagant graciousness in giving us new life in baptism. The symbolism is greatly enhanced if the scent of the *chrism* can be smelled by everyone. In other words, it should be applied liberally enough that this rich symbol is not undercut by timidity.

If there are no baptisms at the Vigil, the Renewal of Baptismal Vows is done instead. The procession to the font follows the sermon. As with the baptismal procession, a litany, psalm, hymn, or anthem may be sung, involving, if possible, the whole congregation.[34] It is also desirable to have the whole congregation follow the procession and gather around the font. Water is poured into the font and a thanksgiving over the water sung, as provided

---

[34] The litany of the saints has been traditionally used as a prayer litany in procession while the baptismal party moves to the font and could be used even if there are no baptisms. It is a means of invoking the presence and prayers of the saints with whom we have communion through Christ. Since in baptism we are bringing new members into that communion, this litany provides a powerful reminder of the universal presence and involvement of the church in this seemingly local event.

on page 330 of the *BAS*. The congregation is invited to renew its baptismal covenant. A short prayer concludes the renewal of vows. If the congregation is to be sprinkled with water from the font, this would appropriately take place after the baptismal covenant and before the short concluding prayer.

When the baptisms or renewal of vows are completed, the rest of the eucharistic liturgy continues in the usual way, with the peace and the reception of Easter communion. Congregations might consider allowing the Paschal Candle to burn from the end of the Vigil until after the last Easter Sunday liturgy is completed.

A Further Note on Structure

As stated previously, there are a number of possible arrangements for the various parts of the Great Vigil. Each arrangement may be given a particular rationale, and it is important to reflect on why a particular choice may be made. In addition to the order outlined above, the *BAS* provides for another ordering.

The church is in darkness, and the service begins with the introduction to the Liturgy of the Word. The pattern of reading, psalm, and collect is followed, with light provided only at the lectern (and perhaps candles held by the congregation with which to read music). In this liturgical sequence, history is "re-enacted" — the story of the Israelites' (and our) passage from slavery to freedom being recounted before the light of Christ is proclaimed.

There are, of course, no official Anglican formularies that contain this litany. Even in the Roman rite, the litany of the saints is used very occasionally in the liturgy. As most Anglicans have no experience of invoking the prayers of the saints, or have theological reasons for *not* doing so, it is unlikely that many parishes will choose this option. The Prayers for the Candidates in the baptismal rite, however, may be sung while processing to the font.

When the readings are completed (after the last reading, psalm, and collect), the Service of Light begins with the kindling of the new fire. After the *Exsultet* has been sung, the liturgy continues with the Easter Acclamation or Hymn of Praise, and the Collect of the Day, followed by the eucharist with baptism or the renewal of vows in the usual place after the sermon.

THE GREAT FIFTY DAYS

The Sundays of Eastertide

"This is the day the Lord has made" — a day far other than those made at the creation of the world which are measured by the passage of time. This day is the beginning of another creation, for on this day God made a new heaven and a new earth as the prophet says. What heaven? The firmament of the faith we have in Christ. What earth? The good heart which is like earth, that drinks the rain that descends on it and brings forth varied fruit.

St. Gregory of Nyssa, Ad 1 on the Resurrection

Colour: White

While the first eucharist of Easter is at the Great Vigil, popular piety is likely to continue to see the Sunday of the Resurrection as *the* Easter celebration for some time to come. There is certainly no reason to undercut the enthusiasm and festivity of Easter Day, as long as care is taken to teach people, year after year, about the significance of the Great Vigil and to celebrate it with as much energy, imagination, and care as possible. Even then, however, after the intensity of Lent and the celebration of the *Triduum*, it is all too easy to forget that Easter is *a season of celebration* that extends over fifty days. Planning for this season needs to begin well in advance, so that the time of preparation does not in practice overshadow the feast for which everyone was preparing in the first place!

Eastertide can be thought of as one Great Sunday, rather than a series of Sundays or little Easters. A period of time equalling seven squared (in fact, a seventh of the year), Eastertide relates to the whole year as Sunday relates to the week. In the first centuries of the church, candidates for baptism, as well as the faithful, prepared for the Easter sacraments with fasting on Good Friday and Holy Saturday. During the Easter season, however, fasting, and even *kneeling* to pray, were positively outlawed.[35]

Just as the liturgies of Holy Week came to commemorate particular events in the last days of the Lord, so too a similar historicizing of Eastertide occurred. Originally, the Great Fifty Days, the *Pentecosté*, was a unitive celebration. In time, however, such "moments" as the Ascension came to be commemorated on the fortieth day after Easter. The fiftieth day ceased to be the climax of the season, and became instead an occasion for remembering the event of the outpouring of the Spirit. Further, the rise in the popularity of infant baptism meant that the Vigils of Easter and Pentecost (not to mention the Epiphany) ceased to be primary times for baptism. As a result, the baptismal character of the entire year was seriously weakened, while the connection between the Paschal Mystery and the celebration of the sacrament was severed.

With the recent liturgical reforms, Eastertide again becomes the baptismal season *par excellence*. It begins with baptism at the Vigil, and concludes with a baptismal festival on the Day of Pentecost. The lections provide material for the mystagogical instruction of the newly baptized. That is, just as the lectionary during Lent encourages and instructs the candidates preparing for baptism, so during Eastertide preaching can unfold the splendours of the mystery into which they have now entered. This arrangement of catechesis, baptism, and mystagogy reflects the custom of the early church but is as contemporary as the latest practices in adult learning theory. The assumption is that one moves from experience to reflection, rather than the other way around. If people have had opportunity for serious formation in the Christian life, and if the celebration of baptism at the Vigil is powerful and dramatic, the newly baptized will be fairly crying out for a chance to reflect on what they have gone through.

---

[35] Council of Nicaea, Canon 20. This ecumenical council took place in the year 325.

For the preacher, this is an excellent opportunity to continue the dialogue that presumably has been going on for some time with the candidates. Preachers may find a number of ways to include insights from the experience of the newly baptized in Easter sermons. In some cases, candidates themselves may be invited to speak about their spiritual journey. The baptismal character of the season can be further emphasized by leaving the font open and filled with water (to which salt has been added to avoid the risk of things growing).

In order to accentuate the unity of the season, Sundays are now referred to as Sundays *of* Easter rather than *after* Easter. The first reading each Sunday is taken from Acts, in which we hear accounts of the life, growth, and witness of the early church. However idealized a portrait this may be, one cannot help but be refreshed by these stories of the vitality and joy of the early communities. Many insights are offered into the nature of community living. The Acts readings offer themselves as entry points into considerations of our stewardship. How do we share our resources of time, energy, and money with one another and the world? In our country, by the end of April — thanks to Revenue Canada — everyone knows exactly how much money they have made the year before. With the season heading toward mission at Pentecost, there is possibility for thorough catechesis about stewardship, as well as what might prove to be an opportune time for pledges.

The second reading is drawn from either 1 Peter, 1 John, or Revelation, writings that evince joyful faith and confident hope. Some scholars hold that 1 Peter is itself an example of early post-baptismal instruction.[36] Whether or not this is true, the expression, "we have been born anew to a living hope" (1:3), sums up the outlook of the whole epistle. The letter urges its hearers to live out in the present the holiness they received in their baptism.

---

[36] See the summary in Troy Martin, *Metaphor and Composition in 1 Peter* (Atlanta: Scholars Press, 1992), SBL Dissertation Series, 131.

The readings from 1 John generally complement the Gospel reading. Themes of mutual indwelling and love can be explored by preachers.

The readings from Revelation do not easily lend themselves to homiletical exposition. Most are doxologies sung by the host of heaven. The note of praise is obviously consonant with Eastertide, and this glimpse of the heavenly liturgy reminds us that our earthly worship is surrounded and drawn to that of the saints in glory.

The gospels for the Second and Third Sundays of Easter relate appearances of the risen Christ. The Fourth Sunday focuses on Christ as the Good Shepherd who now cares for new members of his flock. The Fifth, Sixth, and Seventh Sundays feature excerpts from the farewell discourses of Jesus according to the Gospel of John. These readings provide material for reflection on the Spirit-filled life of the community and lead toward the culmination of the season at Pentecost.

The Ascension is a festival *within* Easter, celebrating the risen Christ as the one who is Lord of all and who will come again. Thus, there is no longer a separate season of Ascension.

Pentecost, too, should no longer be seen as an isolated feast with its own octave. Rather, the gift of the Spirit is intimately linked to the resurrection and ascension of the Lord. The red vestments are a holdover from the time that Pentecost was kept as a separate festival. Innocent III (d. 1216) had already interpreted that colour as an allusion to the tongues of fire at the Spirit's descent.[37] Planners might well consider continuing to use white vestments on Pentecost to underline the unity of the whole season.

Another feature of the old calendar was Rogationtide. The vagaries of the Canadian climate are such that it is impossible to legislate one national date for either planting or harvest. Thus, both Rogation Days and Harvest Thanksgiving are celebrated according to local custom. In some parts of the country, first

---

37 *De Sacro Altaris Mysterio* I, 65 (PL 217:299 ff.)

plantings will take place during Eastertide. Earth Day is kept at the end of April by many within and without the church. A parish might plan a special celebration to incorporate some of that day's concerns with traditional rogation readings and observances.

The Paschal Candle, as a pre-eminent symbol of the Risen Christ among his people, needs to be planned for and purchased well in advance. It should be of sufficient size that it can easily be seen in the building, and have the capacity to burn until the end of the season. The diameter of the candle stand will affect, of course, the size of the candle you can buy or make.[38] In the *Exsultet* at the Great Vigil, the deacon prays that the "Morning Star which never sets find this flame still burning." It is important, then, that the Paschal Candle be found burning as people arrive for any liturgy throughout the season, and that it be extinguished only after the faithful have left the building.

What of Easter Day and its celebration within the context of the Great Fifty Days? Perhaps, eventually, the vast majority of faithful will attend the Easter Vigil as *the* liturgy that both ends the *Triduum* and begins the Easter season. Evening Prayer might then be the other celebration on Easter Sunday. Until that time, however, the liturgy will have to be celebrated on Easter morning.

Elements of the Vigil celebration will persist through Easter Day as well as throughout the season. There should be a heightened solemnity and joy. Extra flowers, the finest vestments, incense, banners, and other decorations are entirely appropriate according to parish custom. The Paschal Candle should be prominently displayed, and may be surrounded by flowers throughout the season. The font should contain water. While a baptism on Easter Sunday is probably outside the experience of many, especially of

---

38 A community might wish to make its own candle rather than approach a religious goods supplier. See the article by Fr. Jonathan Scalone found in the January/February 1981 issue of *Liturgy 80* and reprinted in Gabe Huck, *The Three Days — Parish Prayer in the Paschal Triduum* (Chicago: Liturgy Training Publications, 1981), 113-118.

the more occasional worshippers, such an event could bear eloquent witness to resurrection faith. Care should be taken to make parents, sponsors, and candidates visible, perhaps including them in the entrance procession. If there are no baptisms, a renewal of baptismal vows may be made and the congregation sprinkled with water from the font.

Easter Day is an occasion to ensure that children are most welcome. If their preparation for the day included making Easter eggs, be sure to bless them during the liturgy. Some of the eggs might join Easter bread and other refreshments as part of the hospitality offered after the service.

The Vigil of the Resurrection for Saturday Evenings

What a strange and astonishing situation! We did not really die, we were not really buried, we did not really hang from a cross and rise again. Our imitation was symbolic, but our salvation a reality. Christ truly hung from a cross, was truly buried, and truly rose again. All this he did gratuitously for us, so that we might share his sufferings by imitating them, and gain salvation in actuality. What boundless love! The innocent hands and feet of Christ were pierced by the nails: he suffered the pain. I suffer neither pain nor anguish: yet by letting me participate in his pain he gives me the free gift of salvation. No one should think, then, that his baptism is merely for the remission of sins and for adoption as children in the way that John's baptism brought only remission of sins. We know well that not merely does it cleanse sins and bestow on us the gift of the Holy Spirit — it is also the counterpart of Christ's suffering. This is why, as we heard just now, Paul cried out: "Do you not know that all of us who have been baptized into Christ Jesus were baptized into his death? We were buried therefore with him by baptism into death."

From the instructions to the newly baptized at Jerusalem, Myst 2,4–6

Colour: White

Unlike the secular day, the Christian day (like its Jewish antecedent) begins not with the alarm clock but with the praise of God. Beginning at sundown rather than dawn, the liturgical day starts at a time when a kind of Sabbath rest steals over creation. The fullest celebrations of the new day come at the Sabbath for Jews and on Sunday for Christians. For Anglicans, the memory of this manner of dividing days has been preserved by celebrating days of note with a "first evensong."

The Vigil of the Resurrection is a service that celebrates the beginning of Sunday as the Day of Resurrection. First evensongs notwithstanding, the idea of beginning the day at sundown is likely to be unfamiliar to most Anglicans. The service of the Vigil of the Resurrection has no Anglican antecedents, though it incorporates elements of vigil services dating back to fourth-century Jerusalem. Accordingly, to celebrate this liturgy is both a challenge and an opportunity. In the first place, the pastor will have to introduce people to the idea of an evening service as the beginning of the new day. There is also the challenge of proposing that people come together to worship on a Saturday evening, a time when there are usually myriad distracting entertainments, or simply fatigue, at the end of the day's and week's tasks.

On the other hand, the Resurrection Vigil on Saturday offers the opportunity to celebrate another dimension of Sunday as the day of Resurrection. If the Resurrection Vigil is used during Eastertide, people will see that it bears many resemblances to the Great Vigil. Indeed, after celebrating the Saturday evening vigil for a time, just why the Great Vigil of Easter is so named becomes a whole lot clearer. Further, Eastertide is long enough to let newcomers to the rite get to know it fairly well, yet not so long as to stretch into an impossibly extended commitment for overburdened people or clergy.

While this service may be used on any Saturday evening of the year, Eastertide may be a good time to introduce it. People already view Lent as a season to make extra effort in study or worship, and might appreciate experiencing Eastertide, too, as a season for spiritual growth.

(The Vigil of the Resurrection should probably not be used during Lent. A celebration of Evening Prayer that is Lenten in tone would be more suitable for Saturdays during that season. Notwithstanding the fact that Sundays are always feasts of the resurrection, our experience during Lent is not centred on the singing of Alleluia with which the Resurrection Vigil is replete.)

Items Needed for the Service

- altar vested in colour of the Sunday
- alb or cassock and surplice
- Paschal Candle and stand
- hand candles for congregation during service of light
- ewer of water at the font
- [*aspergillum* or branch for sprinkling of congregation]
- [thurible and incense]

The Service of Light

The rubric indicates that the service *may* begin after the Service of Light (as found on pp. 61–65). In fact, it is strongly recommended that the Service of Light *always* be used with the Vigil, making the connection with the Great Vigil much clearer. During Eastertide, Thanksgiving number 7, "Resurrection," is used (p. 65). The rubrics also indicate that before this service there should be "as little artificial light as possible." As a practical necessity for people who must find seats, service books, and possibly tapers, it is advisable to have some lights on at the entrance.

Because, realistically, this service is not going to be attended by a great many people, thought might be given to the possibility of rearranging the furnishings to provide a more intimate space. If that is impossible, the congregation might be invited to sit in the choir, a smaller chapel, or another room altogether. Because this service allows for movement from one place to another (for example, from the place where the Gospel is read to the font), it will be important to clear the pathway of any obstacles to allow people to move as freely as possible. Again, a situation in which pews tend to be a liability!

After everyone has gathered, the lights can be extinguished and a generous period of darkness enjoyed, to allow the congregation to make the transition from the busyness of the day to worship. One of the ministers then lights the Paschal Candle, or (as the rubrics say) another large candle or, during Advent, an Advent wreath. Note that, if this service is celebrated over a period of weeks (during Eastertide for example), darkness will give way to longer daylight hours. The time of the service should be set with this in mind. On the other hand, by the time Pentecost arrives, there is the lovely possibility that the entire service might be celebrated without any artificial light at all.

If the gathering is to be a small one, it might be possible to group chairs in a circle or semi-circle with the Paschal Candle in the midst. The candle would stand before the lectern from which the Thanksgiving for Light and the Gospel would be read.

Rather than having to light the Paschal Candle from a match or small taper, a minister could carry it, already lit, into the room. Alternatively, a small taper might be lit from a candle that burns perpetually in the church — the sanctuary lamp, for example. From the large candle, small hand tapers held by members of the congregation may be lit. When all the candles are alight, the *Phos Hilaron* (p. 61) is sung. If there is no available musical setting of this hymn as translated in the *BAS*, another translation may be used, such as "O gladsome light, O grace," "Hail gladdening Light, of his pure glory poured," or the metrical version on page 690 of the *BAS*. There is no warrant for reciting the hymn.

In places where incense is used, it should be burned, possibly in a brazier set before the Paschal Candle, during the singing of the *Phos Hilaron*. The rubrics for the Service of Light suggest using all or part of Psalm 141 while incense is offered (p. 65), but because of the shape of the rest of the Vigil, Psalm 141 would seem an unnecessary addition. If a thurible is used, the candle is censed, and then members of the congregation. In a small gathering it is possible to bow before each person before honouring him or her with incense.

Psalmody

Everyone is seated while Psalm 118 is sung or said. This psalm, prominent in the *kerygma* of the early church, takes up the theme of the rejected one being vindicated by God. If it is too difficult for the congregation to sing all of the psalm, a setting might be found that offers the people an Alleluia as a refrain to verses sung by a cantor or small choir.

After the psalm, everyone stands to pray at the officiant's invitation. After a period of silent prayer, the prayer on page 134 is offered.

The Resurrection Gospel

Still standing, all sing or say Psalm 150. Every effort should be made to find some musical setting for this psalm so that it may be sung by everyone, because it serves as a congregational acclamation before the Gospel.

One of the accounts of the resurrection suggested on page 135 is read. It is announced in the usual manner: "The Holy Gospel of our Lord Jesus Christ according to N." If the community is accustomed to singing (or saying) responses before and after the Gospel at the eucharist, they may do so here.

Thanksgiving for Water

The Thanksgiving for Water is an optional part of this rite. When the Thanksgiving is done, it emphasizes connections with the Easter Vigil and encourages a sense of Eastertide as a time of celebrating our participation through baptism in the Paschal Mystery. The Thanksgiving may be said or sung. Music for the Thanksgiving may be found on page 18 of the sacramentary.

This Thanksgiving is best offered at the font. The congregation should gather around, or as near as possible to, the font. If the service must be held in another room where access to the font is impossible, it will be necessary to have a large container for water available. Water is poured into the font (or container) just before the Thanksgiving is offered. At the conclusion of the Thanksgiving, the congregation could be sprinkled with the water as a sign of their participation in the baptismal covenant. Alternatively, people may be invited to dip their fingers in the water and sign themselves, or one another, with the cross. The Canticle of Moses may follow as a further expression of thanks for our deliverance from the bondage of sin and death. Because a canticle is a song, it should be sung rather than recited.

Conclusion

The rite concludes with some versicles and responses, a prayer, and an extended blessing. A musical setting for this section may be found in *Praise God in Song*, published by GIA Publications, Inc., Chicago. As the text is somewhat different, some adjustments will be necessary. There is no dismissal as such — which may be disconcerting to congregations accustomed to hearing this indication that the service is over. Either the officiating minister(s) will have to give the lead in departing, or else an Easter dismissal could be added. It is to be hoped that future redactions of the *BAS* will include a dismissal for this service.

The Vigil of Pentecost

The water that I shall give him will become in him a spring of water welling up to eternal life." This is a new kind of water, living, welling up, welling up for those who are worthy. Why did he call the grace of the Spirit water? Because all things depend on water. Water produces herbs and living things. Water comes down from heaven as rain: water always comes down in the same form, yet its effects are manifold — thus it takes one form in the palm tree and another in the vine; it is in all things and takes all forms, though it is uniform and always remains itself. For the rain does not change, coming down now as one thing and now as another, but it adapts itself to the nature of things which receive it and it becomes what is appropriate to each.

Similarly with the Holy Spirit. He is one and of one nature and indivisible, but he apportions his grace as he wills to each one. When the dry tree is watered it brings forth shoots. So too the soul in sin: when through penance it is made worthy of the grace of the Holy Spirit, it bears the fruits of justice. Though the Spirit is one in nature, yet by the will of God and in the name of Christ he brings about multiple effects of virtue.

From the instructions of St. Cyril of Jerusalem to catechumens, Cat 16

The only provision given in the *BAS* for the Eve of Pentecost is to be found in the psalms and readings for Evening Prayer (p. 468). Being a special way to celebrate the end of the Paschal season, however, this vigil may add a new dimension to the parish's worship. A vigil is a way of expressing our longing for the gracious mystery to be celebrated. An atmosphere of prayerful attention is developed by the elements of darkness, light, readings, silence, and prayer. To begin to appreciate anything of the splendid sweep of the mystery we celebrate, our spirits need to be loosened, stretched, and quietened until a relaxed and centred state of attention to the Word of God is established. This takes time. It requires creativity to provide the elements in the right balance for those who are to attend. A vigil on the eve of Pentecost may be a final time of prayerful preparation for baptismal candidates and their families, or simply an opportunity to celebrate the church's call to Spirit-filled mission.

The following is an account of what one parish, in company with its deanery, attempted. It may be a stimulus to the creativity of others.

St. Stephen-in-the-Fields is a small church in downtown Toronto. The "fields" are now only metaphorical. When it was built, the busy street outside its door did not exist. Long since swallowed up by the city, St. Stephen's congregation has changed considerably as a result of the vast shifts in the makeup of the surrounding ethnic population. Following the original English settlers, successive waves of European Jews, Italians, West Indians, Portuguese, and Chinese have changed the character of the neighbourhood. As a result, St. Stephen's draws few people from within its parish boundaries, though the congregation is quite diverse, including many West Indians and some Anglos, Africans, Latinos, and East Indians.

St. Stephen's is a part of Parkdale deanery, many of whose member parishes have faced changes similar to those of St. Stephen: shrinking congregations, declining revenues, mounting costs, ageing buildings. To try to deal with these realities, the deanery held two conferences on urban mission and evangelism as part of an effort to reclaim the parish neighbourhoods. Five years ago, some of the participating churches joined to plan a celebration of the Vigil of Pentecost and to pray for the renewal of their ministries in the downtown area. The congregation was provided with a booklet that included all the music that was to be sung. Although there was no choir, several cantors were on hand to give leadership. With one exception, the singing was entirely *a cappella*.

Since then, the Pentecost Vigil has become an annual and valued part of the celebration of the season, with people continuing to come from a variety of church communities. The Vigil continues to feature *a cappella* singing. Some of the readings have been accompanied by musical instruments. A breathy flute, a rain stick, and some wooden blocks to clatter during the reading of Ezekiel 37 have added much. Other readings have been interpreted in dance, another spirited means of expressing the Word.

As there are no pews in St. Stephen's nave, it is possible to arrange the chairs in a semi-circle. The Paschal Candle stands in the midst of the congregation and before a lectern. When the candle is lit, the presider begins the Service of Light (p. 61). While the *Phos Hilaron* is sung, the candle and the congregation are censed. The form of Thanksgiving for the Resurrection (number 7 on page 65) is sung, with congregational acclamations sung after each section of the prayer.

Then follow the readings. Only five readings are read, in recognition that on a lovely spring evening the congregation might find more excessive. Three of the lections are from Scripture, and two are from modern authors.[39] The Scriptural passages are chosen from the readings for the Great Vigil. The order has been: Ezekiel 37:1–14, silence, Psalm 143, collect; contemporary author, silence; Isaiah 44:1–8, silence, The Song of Thanksgiving, collect; contemporary author, silence; Romans 8:22–27.

Taizé refrains punctuate the psalmody. After the reading from Romans, the Taizé chant "Veni Sancte Spiritus" is sung for an extended period of time. The chant, like the other music, is sung in four parts, but in this instance with the accompaniment of organ, synthesizer, and flute! After the chant is ended, there is an

---

[39] Over the years, these have included Henri Nouwen, Anthony deMello, Dorothy Soelle, Thomas Merton, Hildegaard of Bingen (less modern, but not Scripture!). Planners make an effort to find readings that speak as specifically as possible to current challenges.

extended period of silence, after which everyone rises to hear the Gospel for the Day of Pentecost. The service concludes with the prayers that come from the end of the "Resurrection Vigil" (p. 137).

When this service was first planned, members of the deanery churches decided not to include a celebration of the eucharist, assuming that people would attend the Sunday liturgy in their own parish. We have never altered this. The value of the Vigil of Pentecost is found in the enthusiastic return of people year after year. Highest praise goes to the deep silence that follows ten or fifteen minutes of chanting "Veni Sancte Spiritus."

Music for the Paschal Celebration

Basic Principles

Christian worship is sung worship. The avalanche of new liturgical texts, which at times seems to overwhelm parishes, obscures the fact that music is at the core of our faithful celebration of the liturgy. Think for a moment about the music in the scriptural narratives. Jesus probably sang the ancient *berakah* chant as he blessed the bread and cup at his last supper, and the disciples responded with the great "Hallelujah." He may have sung that same chant at the evening meal at Emmaus after his resurrection. As he entered Jerusalem, did the crowds spontaneously sing their hosanna verses from Psalm 118?

For most Anglican worshippers, music is an integral part of their liturgical experience. The Paschal celebration calls for an even deeper appreciation of the power of music to illuminate the words on the page and create a real dialogue with God. It is no accident that music lovers in record numbers still go to concerts of sacred music at Easter. Liturgical renewal is impossible without a musical renewal in the church. When new liturgies fail, it is often a musical problem. Therefore, we must make music an integral part of liturgical planning. It would be helpful in this regard for non-musicians, both clerical and lay, to stop thinking of music as an "add-on" to a selection of printed texts and for musicians to no longer operate in isolation but, rather, to see their music as expressive of the whole community.

This revision of our traditional "top-down" method of thinking needs to begin long before the Paschal celebration. The period from Lent to Easter is an exhilarating and exhausting journey, and to enter fully into its celebration, parishes are encouraged to develop a process that allows for creative and non-confrontational planning. A few fundamental concepts might be kept in mind when planning for the liturgy of this season.

1. Hear all texts as music: prayers, readings, and psalms. Get out of the five hymn syndrome. Look for places to have more music, not less.
2. Assume congregational participation. Given challenging but accessible music, people will take their rightful role in worship. Music, classical or pop, that denies the people a voice is not liturgical music.
3. Explore new musical sounds. Although the organ remains the fundamental support, a change in musical sonority can be liberating. Wind, string, and percussion instruments can be used in various combinations to create effective liturgical moments.
4. Use silence as music.
5. Experiment with unaccompanied singing. The human voice is the most expressive instrument we have. Even a small group singing alone can be a powerful experience.
6. If you can't find the right music, write your own.

A Final Note

Plan to implement music and liturgical changes over a two- or three-year period. It is difficult to find the creativity and energy to do it all in one year. In practical terms, most parishes might start with Good Friday and move on to the Easter Vigil, the Sunday of the Passion, and Maundy Thursday. When these rites are in place, the parish will have a better perspective from which to build liturgies in Lent and Easter.

Primary Music Resources

The following list is not intended to be comprehensive. It is a practical starting point for parishes who want both continuity and change in their celebrations. It presumes that most music is still supported by the organ and led by a modest choir. These collections will provide basic resources for building the musical sequence for the Paschal celebrations. Churches with a choral tradition, or who have contemporary music groups, will find links to other material.

1. *Common Praise* (1998). This hymn book is an excellent source for Canadian parish worship. The musical selection is conservative and practical, traditional and contemporary, and the editors have performed a great service by providing a full complement of hymns which are linked to the three-year lectionary cycle. The book contains a number of different settings of the common texts of the eucharist and offices.

2. *Voices United* (1995). The new United Church hymn book provides a wide selection of traditional and contemporary hymns. Inclusive language and the exclusion of imperial imagery are hallmarks. Parishes that have used *Songs of a Gospel People* will find similar material here. The thematic organization makes it more difficult for Anglican parishes to use it, but there is a good offering of hymns and songs with social justice and creation theology perspectives. A large selection of metrical and responsorial psalms provides settings for nearly all the requirements of the *BAS*.

3. *Gather* (1994). This Roman Catholic collection offers a full liturgical program for parishes and contains settings of most of the texts in the *BAS*. The musical selection is broad and includes many contemporary songs which have become popular in Anglican churches. The Holy Week and Easter sections have much valuable material. The settings of the eucharist are graded so that parishes will quickly find music suited to their resources.

4. *Music from Taizé* (1984). The music from this ecumenical community in France is a good meeting point for liturgical radicals and conservative church musicians. The music is

fundamentally congregational in nature but challenging to musicians on all levels. Many of the pieces in the two collections are not direct settings of the *BAS* texts. The *ostinato* chants and responsorial pieces complement the liturgical texts and can create a uniquely spiritual, meditative atmosphere.

5. *Gradual Psalms* (1988). This is a resource by George Black for parishes who want to sing the poetry of the psalter. They will find all of the gradual psalms for the *BAS* rite here. The music is written in an approachable Gelineau style with simple congregational refrains and easy solo verses. This collection is an excellent practical base from which to expand and experiment.

6. A *New Metrical Psalter* (1986). Designed as a supplemental resource for *The Book of Common Prayer* of the Episcopal church, this publication gives a complete set of metrical translations for the whole psalter. Each of the psalms lists the metre and suggests two or three traditional hymn tunes. Metrical versions of all the major canticles in the *BAS* are included. The translations are serviceable.

A Note about Copyright

Music publishers do not make it easy for parishes to build up a varied liturgical program. In most cases, parishes simply cannot afford expensive collections. This dilemma, however, does not excuse us from the legal and ethical obligations of responding to copyright. In the past few years, music publishers have finally realized that they are losing their profits to the photocopy machine and have started to provide more realistic solutions. Most publishers now offer licensing arrangements that allow for the reproduction of music leaflets and disposable service booklets. Parishes and deaneries are encouraged to work together in securing their permission. Every diocese in the church should be looking at licensing.

Ash Wednesday

In most parishes, the Ash Wednesday celebration will probably be held in the early evening on a normal business day. Both pastoral and musical considerations call for simplicity and directness. Consider shutting down the organ and singing everything unaccompanied, or perhaps using a flute or violin to provide an accent to the singing. Generous silences — three or four minutes at least! — will provide a powerful element for the opening and conclusion of the liturgy and in the penitential meditation on page 282. Short silences are just liturgical hesitations. In choosing a psalm between the readings, consider introducing a refrain that will be used throughout the season of Lent (Common Refrain 8 on page 266 is suggested). Some musical contrast is in order to emphasize Psalm 51; a metrical version is recommended if the earlier psalm was chanted.

The Litany of Penitence gains immeasurably if sung. The litany responses (pp. 915–917) can be easily adapted to the suggested texts. As a general principle, a short response is more effective if repeated two or three times. This allows the congregation time to hear the music and repeat it. The failure of much modern liturgical music comes from not using the inherent power of repetition, a principle that is manifest in Orthodox music. The time during the imposition of ashes is an example of a moment that calls for a creative response. Filling it up completely with hymns is boring. Use your resources imaginatively: a single solo voice singing a spiritual or an instrumental player improvising are two possibilities.

Sundays in Lent

The challenge of Lent is finding a musical expression that sets it off from both the green season of post-Epiphany and the Great Fifty Days of Easter. We also have to disabuse ourselves of the notion that these are "sad" days and that the music has to be funereal. A close study of the readings will reveal that the scriptural themes are more often arrestingly positive. Music with strong new images is an important resource here, and Lent comes alive when lyrics from other cultures are sung. The publications of the World Council of Churches contain much music that could give Lent a special flavour. A South African hymn or a Middle Eastern song can give the celebration a unique musical texture.

Of all the seasons, Lent suffers most from our dependence on hymns. It is not that singing hymns is inherently wrong, but that the musical sound is too similar to the seasons before and after. In particular, the entrance rite for each Sunday needs careful attention. Try a silent procession, use the traditional Great Litany (p. 110) or instrumental music. If the *Kyrie* or *Trisagion* (pp. 186–187) is used for the Gathering, expand the setting with solo verses so that the congregation has time to assimilate the musical response. The verses of the Lenten litany (p. 121) or the responsory (p. 106) are suitable. Similarly, use a repeated sung response in the Prayers of the People. In combination with well-placed silences, the prayers will take on a depth that the simple recitation of texts cannot achieve.

The Sunday of the Passion

The liturgy of this day has two contrasting themes that need to be expressed and balanced in the music. The first, in the Liturgy of the Palms, is extraverted and triumphal; the second, in the reading of the Passion, is more introspective and intense. Care needs to be taken that the triumphalism of the entry does not overshadow the rest of the liturgy. If the procession of palms goes outside the church, take time to sing the processional song as an introduction to the liturgy, so that the people can learn the music without having to walk at the same time. Choose a solid unison hymn or song that will be effective even if sung without accompaniment — choral harmony is not particularly successful outdoors. Drumming before the liturgy and during the procession is an ideal solution for energizing the community — the Coptic church has known this for centuries! Whichever musical style is chosen, it must have compelling energy, or shy Anglicans will simply opt out. If a repeated "Hosanna" refrain is used, extended percussion or instrumental interludes can provide relief. It is exhausting to sing continuously outdoors. Pace the music. The Liturgy of the Word can also be integrated with the procession. The short prophetic reading from Isaiah can be declaimed at the church door, and the second reading from Philippians can then be sung as a metrical hymn, "All Praise to Christ," as the procession enters the church. This passage was originally a hymn.

The shift to the reading of the Gospel needs some sensitivity, especially if the palm procession has been exciting and extraverted. A significant silence or a repeated Taizé chant such as, "Jesu, remember me," will help to lower the liturgical temperature, as well as give Canadian worshippers a chance to shed coats and warm up! If the Passion Gospel is read, it should be treated as music and rehearsed accordingly. The narrative would be better read by one well-prepared reader than divided among a large number of indifferent voices. The responses of the crowd are much more effective if repeated two or three times; for example,

> Crowd *(growing louder each time)*: Not this man, but Barabbas! Not this man, but Barabbas!! Not this man, but Barabbas!!!

Creative use of instruments and sounds during the Passion Gospel can also create an effective soundscape. A muffled drum during the march to Calvary, a metal hammer striking nails for the crucifixion, and a stamping of feet for the earthquake can be dramatic musical support for the reading. This type of musical reading requires good planning and adequate rehearsal.

A final consideration for the conclusion of the liturgy of Passion Sunday: too often the triumphalism of the palm procession returns and seems to isolate the celebration from the rest of Holy Week. A sense of open-endedness needs to be created so that the way points ahead to the Last Supper and the Garden of Gethsemane. Unaccompanied singing and silence might be effective ways of bringing the celebration to a quiet but expectant end.

Maundy Thursday

Like Ash Wednesday, Maundy Thursday will be celebrated on an extremely busy working day (five days' work crammed into four for the holiday). This point is emphasized because it is easy for liturgists to lose sight of the fact that we are planning worship for parish churches, not cathedrals or monastic communities. As on Ash Wednesday, the celebration should have a quiet simplicity that allows working people to enter easily into the devotion.

The character of Maundy Thursday is still controverted among liturgical scholars, and a parish's choice of music will reflect their point of view. For many, the focus is on the washing of feet; for others, it is the institution of the eucharist. For the latter, the celebration will have something of a festal occasion: the liturgy can be concelebrated, bells may be rung while the Gloria is sung as a canticle for the Gathering of the Community. Other communities may prefer to use the *Trisagion* with verses and to keep the atmosphere more circumscribed.

If the washing of feet is the central focus of the celebration, the act can be realized in a number of ways, from the highly ritualized washing of a symbolic twelve people's feet in the sanctuary to an informal activity involving everyone in the church. The rite will take as long as the distribution of communion, and the musical sequence needs to be balanced and varied so that worshippers are not wearied by a long series of hymns. The "Ubi Caritas" of the Taizé community is highly recommended because of its flexibility in using repeated refrains, solo verses, and instrumental interludes. Organ and instrumental music can also offer a variety of sonority.

In parishes where communion is given from the reserved sacrament on Good Friday, there may be a need for a hymn as the sacrament is taken from the church or to a side altar. "Now my tongue" is the traditional text. However, the concluding rite should not overshadow the foot washing, and the music chosen should be simple, perhaps unaccompanied. The stripping of the altar(s) is essentially a domestic activity outside the liturgy, but the old prejudice of prohibiting instrumental music until Easter Eve is neither practical nor desirable. In fact, the stripping, as well as a watch vigil through Thursday night, might well use music to provide a context for silent devotion. Music from the Friday Vigil of the Taizé community, and organ or instrumental music, would meet a real spiritual need, even if it lies outside the official rites.

Good Friday

The renewed celebration of Good Friday presents something of a dilemma for church musicians. In the past, following a tradition going back to the Lutheran Bach and Catholic Haydn, Good Friday has been the occasion for a great deal of fine music-making, usually in the form of a concert of choral music. In many parishes, this concert is the most important event in Holy Week and frequently draws people who will not appear again on Easter. If this tradition is operative, it will take much consultation to move the musical energy to the new liturgy. It is absolutely essential that this be achieved by consensus, so that there is never competition between liturgy and concert.

In practical terms, planners will have to work hard to find a model that can accommodate the very real need of musicians to honour the season with good music outside the liturgy, and the desire of historical liturgists to impose an artistic austerity on the day. Neither extreme is productive. In all of these situations, we have to look at the pastoral situation and ask what will provide the access point for the worshipper. The needs of the local church have to take precedence over uniformity. The opening of the Good Friday liturgy is a good example. The *BAS* mandates silence for the entrance. Silence is an essential component of good liturgy, but is it inherently superior to a Bach organ chorale or a soloist singing, "Were you there"? Some might say that all three should be part of the rite.

The potential for music-drama in the reading of the Passion Gospel has been discussed earlier in the section on the Sunday of the Passion. The same holds true for the Passion on Good Friday.

To these resources we may add the possibility of extended musical settings of the Passion (the Bach Passions were, after all, originally liturgical works). In all cases, the question of balance and the participation of the congregation need to be primary concerns.

The greatest scope for musical participation is in the Meditation on the Cross of Jesus. The *BAS* ordo is particularly unhelpful for this, albeit, optional part of the rite. The vagueness of the *BAS* provision has something to do with a traditional Anglican reluctance to honour representations of Christian symbols such as the cross. There is a reluctance, as well, to use texts such as Anthem 1, "The Reproaches," on page 314 that, although rigorously revised here, have been the locus of much historic anti-Semitism.

Given the formlessness of the *BAS* provisions here and later in the distribution of the communion, the rite will be shaped by the musical sequence. The first part of the Meditation is the procession of the cross into the church. Following the dramatic traditional usage, the dialogue, "This is the wood of the cross," is sung three times to the simple response tone, each time at a higher pitch. Although silence between the repetitions is effective, there is also the equally dramatic possibility of the dialogue interrupting the sections of a song or hymn.

Anthem 1 is available in many settings, both traditional and contemporary, although parishes that have sung the *Trisagion* during Lent may wish to use it a last time here, the verses being sung by the choir or soloist. If the Meditation includes a movement of the people forward to touch or kiss the cross, one of the repeated *ostinato* refrains from the Friday Evening Office of the Passion by the Taizé community would free people from having printed material in their hands. Anthems 2 through 4 could be used in place of Anthem 1. *Gather* has the largest number of settings for these texts. And again, there is nothing to prevent other texts from being used in the place of these anthems, although care must be taken not to lay on a long series of hymns.

The Meditation traditionally concludes with the hymn, "Sing my tongue," during which the altar is prepared for communion.

Again, a string of hymns should be avoided during the distribution (as it should at every eucharist). This is an opportunity for a creative sequence that employs congregational, choral, solo, and instrumental music.

The Great Vigil of Easter

As Easter is the centre of the church year, so the musical program for the Vigil should in its scope and preparation display the centrality of the Saturday evening liturgy. The Easter Vigil brings together liturgies that once stretched from sunset on Saturday to dawn on Sunday. As such, there is an enormous amount of music to put in place for this rite. Parishes would do well to build their resources over two or three years, rather than try to do everything at once. It is also important to discover the parish's liturgical stamina. Less is always better at the beginning.

The Service of Light

There are few musical experiences more satisfying than the simple versicle and response for "The Light of Christ," sung three times, each time a half-tone higher, as the procession comes into the church with the Paschal Candle. The chant of the *Exsultet* that follows is historically the prerogative of the deacon. It is, however, a challenge to sing, and clergy might well share it with one or two strong singers, reserving to the deacon the section from "The Lord be with you" to the bottom of page 323, and the doxology from "Therefore, heavenly Father" to the bottom of page 324. The traditional recitation tone should be used if the singer is confident and has the musical stamina. Simpler versions are available, and a judicious mix is sometimes preferable. There are also settings in which the congregation punctuates the sections with a repeated refrain, such as "Christ is risen" or "Alleluia." These settings are more expressive for the community and provide good musical support for the cantor.

It is also worth discussing here the traditional prohibition against using the organ and instruments until the Gloria. Delaying the use of the organ and bells until halfway through the liturgy creates a wonderfully theatrical moment, but the notion that Easter begins with the Gloria does not make sense after the lighting and blessing of the Paschal Candle. Psychologically, the celebration of Easter has begun. Therefore, musicians and planners should not feel constrained against using instruments in any part of the liturgy. A set of handbells would be a superb musical accompaniment to the *Exsultet*. If the effect of each sound picture is carefully considered, then the music will illuminate each part of the rite.

The Liturgy of the Word

The sequence of readings at the Vigil is a magnificent pageant of Scripture, and offers musicians a tantalizing array of opportunities for proclaiming and responding to the stories. Each reading is followed by a responsorial psalm with a congregational refrain. There is a good selection of settings in the publications listed above, and some variety of styles is desirable. One psalm might be chanted responsorially while another is sung metrically. Some parishes might want to simplify the psalms by using one refrain, such as a simple "Alleluia" for all the psalms. An even simpler arrangement would be to use metrical versions sung to one or two familiar hymn tunes. The addition of instruments can change the sound colour in attractive and arresting ways.

Musicians will find it a stimulating experience to work with directors and actors in dramatizing some of the readings. The first reading from Genesis has a marvellous poetic structure that begs for musical realization. The seven days of creation could be taken by seven readers and the people sing the repeated verse, "And God saw that it was good," as a refrain. Each day could be characterized by contrasting sonorities of wind, string, and percussion instruments.

Other readings have dramatic possibilities as well. The story of Abraham and Isaac is a superb scene for three actors — the angel might even sing its part! The account of the Exodus through the Red Sea is a vivid narrative, and the Song of Moses should spring out of the action. The musical march of the Israelites could begin as the reader concludes the final verses and the people respond with their triumphal song. The potential for exciting narrative dramas arises when word and music are wedded.

Holy Baptism

The Easter Vigil presupposes that adult candidates for baptism will be presented. If not, the Renewal of Baptismal Vows takes place (p. 330). If the candidates are infants, the entire Vigil and its music will have to be reconsidered. It is simply impossible to offer an extended musical program and expect families to deal with young children. Pastoral considerations should always take precedence.

Although the subject of music at baptism is a topic in itself, there are a number of places where the music can enliven the celebration. The Prayers for the Candidates (p. 155) gain breadth and dignity when sung to Tone 1 on page 915 of the *BAS*. The text adapts easily to "Lord, have mercy." The response is most effective when sung three times, not just once. The Thanksgiving over the Water (p. 156) is easily sung to the traditional chant of the Eucharistic Prayer. Another option is to sing it to the simpler Tone 1 while the people sing the repeated acclamation, "Blessed be God" or a more familiar "Alleluia." This acclamation can also be used after each baptism and each *chrismation*, so that the liturgical action will be highlighted by music. The use of handbells gives a splendid sense of joy and celebration.

Eucharist

After so much splendid ceremonial and music, the eucharist runs the risk of seeming anti-climatic. One of the arguments in support of not using the organ and bells until the Gloria is that it gives the whole celebration a well-needed boost. In any case, the eucharist needs to have a new colour in the voices or instruments. An unexpected fanfare of trumpets will galvanize a congregation. A familiar setting of the Gloria should be used so that there is a real sense of "homecoming" in the celebration. Even an old war-horse like the Merbecke Gloria can be transformed by handbells.

A Final Note about Easter

The Book of Alternative Services presumes that the Vigil is the central rite of the Paschal celebration. In the vast majority of parishes, the eucharist on Easter Day will continue to be the principal celebration, and some accommodation needs to be made so that the magnificent features of the Vigil are made available to the Sunday morning liturgy. It took nearly a century for the midnight eucharist on Christmas Eve to achieve normative status, and it is not certain that some of the new rites will gain acceptance unless flexibility and renewal are part of our approach. Parish planners and musicians have the responsibility to be creative and to respond to the needs of their particular community. The *BAS* has restored the possibility of passion, colour, and depth in our worship. Now our worship must find its voice in song.

Glossary

Acolyte or server

A lay person who assists the priest and deacon at the altar.

Agnus Dei (Latin: lamb of God)

The hymn beginning with the words, "Lamb of God," sung or recited during the breaking of the bread before the communion.

Apostolic Greeting

The greeting of the Apostle Paul recorded in 2 Corinthians 13:14, "The grace of our Lord Jesus Christ, and the love of God, and the fellowship of the Holy Spirit be with you all."

Asperges (Latin: sprinkle)

The word comes from Psalm 50:9 (also Psalm 51:7) in the Vulgate Psalter: "Thou shalt sprinkle me with hyssop and I shall be cleansed: thou shalt wash me and I shall be made whiter than snow." In the Roman rite, this verse is sung while holy water is sprinkled over the people at the beginning of Mass. An aspergillum or aspersorium is the sprinkler used for the purpose.

Berakah (Hebrew: blessing)

The characteristic Jewish prayer that takes the form of a blessing or thanksgiving to God.

Catechesis

Instruction and formation in Christian teaching and life, used especially in connection with the pre-baptismal training of adults. Those being instructed and informed in Christian teaching and life are known as catechumenates.

Celebration of the Eucharist

In the *BAS*, that section of the eucharistic liturgy that begins with the preparation of the gifts and concludes with the prayer after communion.

Ciborium (Greek: a cup shaped like the seed vessel of a water-lily)

A chalice-shaped vessel, with lid, used to contain wafers for the eucharist.

Concelebration

The practice of a number of bishops or priests participating in the eucharistic prayer in addition to the presiding celebrant. Concelebrants may share in the recitation of the prayer and/or shared gestures during the prayer. In the more ancient pattern, the concelebrants simply stood in physical proximity to the presider.

The Didache (Greek: teaching)

This brief handbook on Christian morals and practice is of unknown date and authorship. It is generally assigned to the first century. It provides much detail about early Christian liturgy.

The Gathering of the Community

The first section of the eucharistic liturgy in the *BAS*. While the ritual material for this action begins with the apostolic greeting and concludes with the Collect of the Day, this part of the liturgy includes everything that happens, from welcome at the door to distribution of service leaflets, as people gather in the building in order to worship together.

Gloria or Glory to God (Latin: Gloria in Excelsis Deo, "Glory to God in the highest")

Sometimes known as the "Greater Doxology" or the "Angelic Hymn" (since it quotes the Angels in Luke 2), this hymn is of unknown authorship and age. It has been part of the eucharistic liturgy of the Western church since roughly the eighth century. In *The Book of Alternative Services*, it is one of the options for an act of praise suitable for beginning the eucharist.

Kerygma (Greek: preaching)

This is proclamation of the Christian message as opposed to instruction or exhortation.

Kyrie Eleison (Greek: Lord, have mercy)

One of the hymns provided in the *BAS* (pp. 186 and 231) for the beginning of the eucharist. This invocation is found in nearly all the historic liturgies. It was used originally as the response to a litany. In the Western church, the intercessory litany that came after the introit of the mass disappeared by the end of the eighth century, with the acclamations alone remaining.

Lex orandi, lex credendi (Latin)

This is generally translated as "the law of prayer is the law of belief." In the introduction to the *BAS* the point is made that this principal means "that theology as the statement of the church's belief is drawn from the liturgy, i.e., from the point at which the gospel and the challenge of life meet in prayer" (p. 10). This short phrase is derived from the theologian Prosper of Aquitaine (*c.* 390 to *c.* 463).

Liturgical Colours

The sequence of colours (usually white, red, green, purple and blue) for use during the seasons and festivals of the church year. A standardized pattern did not come into being in the Western church until the later Middle Ages.

Liturgy of the Sacrament

See "Celebration of the Eucharist."

Liturgy of the Word

See "Proclamation of the Word."

Orans (Latin: Praying)

This is the classic gesture for prayer. One stands with arms upraised. The hands are active, lifting heavenward. In our day, this posture is generally assumed only by the presider, but it was common to all Christians in the first centuries. This is attested to by Clement of Alexandria (d. 215) and by Origen (d.254), who sees in this posture the perfect corporeal expression of prayer:

"Even more than stretching out the hands to heaven, one must lift up the soul heavenward. More than raising the eyes, one must lift up the spirit to God. For there can be no doubt that among a thousand possible positions of the body, outstretched hands and uplifted eyes are to be preferred above all others, so imaging forth in the body those directions of the soul which are fitting in prayer. We are of the opinion that this posture should be preferred, where there is nothing to prevent it, for there are certain circumstances, such as sickness, where we may pray even sitting or lying" *(De Oratione*, 31, 2).

Pasch (Greek: Pascha)

A term referring either to the Jewish festival of Passover or the Christian festival of Easter.

Paschal Mystery or "Easter Mystery"

This phrase refers essentially to the death and resurrection of Christ. Because the gospels associate Jesus' death with the Passover festival, we have come to see the Paschal Mystery as the culmination of God's deliverance of the People of God, first shown in the passage of Israel from slavery in Egypt through the Red Sea to freedom. The Paschal Mystery, then, refers to all that God has done to deliver us from slavery, whether to historical tyrants and systems or to spiritual enemies like sin and death.

The Proclamation of the Word (sometimes known as the Liturgy of the Word)

In the *BAS*, it is the second section of the eucharist, including the reading of Scripture, sermon, creed, and Prayers of the People. It is concluded by the exchange of the Peace.

Quinquagesima (Latin: The Fiftieth [day before Easter])

In *The Book of Common Prayer*, this is the final Sunday before Lent. Ash Wednesday takes place in Quinquagesima week.

Sacramentary

A book used by the presiding celebrant, containing prayers and other texts, as well as music to be used in the celebration.

Sanctus (Latin: Holy)

The hymn that comes after the Preface in the eucharistic prayer, beginning with the words "Holy, holy, holy." As this is a hymn in which the people imitate the praise of the angels, it should be sung rather than recited.

Septuagesima (Latin: The Seventieth [day before Easter])

In *The Book of Common Prayer*, this is the third Sunday before Lent. It marked a stage toward the Lenten fast, with vestments and hangings in purple.

Sexagesima (Latin: The Sixtieth [day before Easter])

In *The Book of Common Prayer*, this is the second Sunday before Lent.

Soteriology (Greek: Soteria, salvation)

That part of Christian theology that deals with Christ's saving work for the world.

Thurible

A metal vessel in which incense is burned. The thurible is suspended by chains, allowing it to be swung. The thurifer is the acolyte who looks after the thurible during a liturgy.

Tract

A chant sung or recited at the eucharist on certain penitential days instead of the Alleluia.

Triduum (Latin: Three Days)

This term refers to the Great Three Days celebrating the Paschal Mystery. Because the liturgical day begins in the evening, the Great Three Days run from the evening of Maundy Thursday to the evening of Easter Sunday. While the term appears nowhere in *The Book of Common Prayer* or in *The Book of Alternative Services*, it is a useful shorthand.

Trisagion (Greek: Thrice Holy)

One of the hymns provided in the *BAS* (pp. 186 and 231) for the beginning of the eucharist. This is a hymn of the Byzantine rite, sung at a point corresponding to the Western "Gloria in Excelsis."

For Further Reading

Balthasar, Hans Urs von, translated with an introduction by Aidan Nichols, *Mysterium Paschale: The Mystery of Easter*. Edinburgh: T & T Clark, 1990.

A major work of theological and devotional reflection on the death and resurrection of Christ by the late Roman Catholic theologian.

Deiss, Lucien, ed. *Springtime of the Liturgy: Liturgical Texts of the First Four Centuries*. Collegeville, Minn.: the Liturgical Press, 1979.

A compendium of liturgical texts from the early church in accessible translation.

Dunn, Greig, *Servers and Services: Instructions for Serving Anglican Liturgies*. Toronto: Anglican Book Centre, 1986.

From Ashes to Easter: Lenten Renewal for the Churches. Centre for Pastoral Liturgy, Catholic University of America. Washington, D.C.: The Liturgical Conference, 1979.

One of the sources of inspiration for the rites of the *BAS*, with practical suggestions for parishes.

From Ashes to Fire: Services of Worship for the Seasons of Lent and Easter. Prepared under the direction of the Board of Discipleship of the United Methodist church. Nashville: Abingdon Press, 1979.

Another of the sources of inspiration for the rites of the *BAS*, with practical suggestions for parishes.

Hamman, A.G., ed. *The Paschal Mystery: Ancient Liturgies and Patristic Texts*. Staten Island, N.Y.: Alba House, 1969.

Another source for those who wish to read the Fathers of the church in translation.

Hatchett, Marion J. *Commentary on the American Prayer Book*. New York: Seabury Press, 1980.

This book offers useful background material to much of the *BAS* because of the many similarities between it and the American book.

Hill, John W.B. *Making Disciples: Serving Those Who Are Entering the Christian Life*. Toronto: The Hoskin Group, 1991.
This is a book with a fresh vision of the way people are prepared for baptism and provides a variety of resources for a renewed catechumenate.

Holeton, David, Catherine Hall and Gregory Kerr-Wilson. *Let Us Give Thanks: A Presider's Guide for the BAS Eucharist*. Toronto: The Hoskin Group, 1991.
A detailed guide to ceremonial.

Huck, Gabe. *The Three Days — Parish Prayer in the Paschal Triduum*. Chicago: Liturgy Training Publications, 1981.
This publication includes directions for making a Paschal Candle, baptismal garments, as well as many other ideas for enriching the season. Refers to the Roman rite.

Reynolds, Stephen. *For All the Saints: Prayers and Readings for Saints' Days*. Toronto: Anglican Book Centre, 1994.

Simcoe, Mary Ann, ed. *Parish Path Through Lent and Eastertime*. Chicago: Liturgy Training Publications, 1985.
A Roman Catholic sourcebook of ideas for the seasons.

Music List

Common Praise: Anglican Church of Canada. Toronto: Anglican Book Centre, 1998.

Voices United: The Hymn and Worship Book of the United Church of Canada. Toronto: United Church Publishing House, 1996.

Gather. Chicago: GIA Publications, 1994.

Berthier, Jacques. *Music from Taizé*. (Brother Robert, ed.) Chicago: GIA Publications, 1984.

Black, George. *Music for the Psalms*. Toronto: Anglican Book Centre, 1988.

Webber, Christopher. *A New Metrical Psalter*. New York: Church Hymnal Corporation, 1986.

Contributors

Douglas Cowling (Music for the Paschal Celebration) is co-author with Paul Maclean of *Sharing the Banquet* and writer of the Juno award-winning series of CDs for *Classical Kids*. He is a member of the Folk Mass Music Group at the church of St. Mary Magdalene, Toronto.

Kevin Flynn (editor, Introduction, Ash Wednesday, Penitential Order, Maundy Thursday, Sundays of Eastertide, The Vigil of the Resurrection, The Vigil of Pentecost) is the incumbent of the church of St. Stephen-in-the-Fields, Toronto, and lecturer in liturgics at Trinity College.

David Holeton (Lent and the New Liturgy: A Pastoral Perspective) is one of the chief framers of *The Book of Alternative Services*. He is professor of liturgy at the Charles University in Prague.

Gregory Kerr-Wilson (Passion Sunday, Monday, Tuesday, and Wednesday in Holy Week, Holy Saturday, The Great Vigil of Easter) is the incumbent of the church of the Holy Family, Brampton.

Robert Ross (Good Friday) is associate priest at the church of St. Thomas, Toronto and the author of *Preparing for Baptism: Using the Book of Alternative Services.*